Cool Camping

Laura James

Cool Camping

Laura James

Collins

First published in 2006 by Collins, an imprint of
HarperCollins Publishers
77-85 Fulham Palace Road
Hammersmith, London W6 8JB

www.collins.co.uk

Collins is a registered trademark of HarperCollins Publishers Limited

07 09 08
3 5 6 4 2

For HarperCollins
Senior Commissioning Editor: Jenny Heller
Editor: Lisa John
Senior Production Controller: Chris Gurney

This book was designed and produced for HarperCollins by
The Mabel Gray Company
Researcher: Zofia Falvey

ISBN-13: 978-0-00-723055-6
ISBN-10: 0-00-723055-9

Colour reproduction by Colourscan, Singapore
Printed and bound by Printing Express Ltd, Hong Kong

☾ Collins

contents

✳ Contributors

24 Martin Miller
31 Kevin McCloud
55 Alex James
57 Emma Bridgewater
62 Hugh Fearnley-Whittingstall
63 Lucy Young
64 Wilfred Emmanuel-Jones
66 Mitchell Tonks
68 Tom Norrington-Davies
71 Raffaella Barker
74 Jodie Kidd
77 Alice Temperley
81 William Higham
101 Emily Eavis
113 Kim Wilde

whycampingiscool

It's fun, fashionable and easy to do with great style.
It offers an unparalleled sense of freedom and
allows you to let your imagination run wild.

Camping is officially cool again. But before you start having nightmares about being trapped in a field with a bus-load of boy scouts, let me explain. Camping has changed a lot. Gone are the days of being stuck next to the couple from hell who can't wait to get you under their awning so they can subject you to two hours of mind-numbing conversation about double-entry book keeping.

Today it's about style, comfort and a sprinkling of glamour. Think Kate Moss at Glastonbury, Airstreams and T@b caravans. Drift off into a fantasy of vintage VW campers, bright white tipis stretching skywards and pretty tents peppered with flowers. Arguably, it was Cath Kidston's delicious floral tent which kicked off the latest camping craze.

Imagine sitting round the campfire, eating delicious food and telling ghost stories. Think boys in feather headdresses and girls with fairy wings. This is today's camping experience.

Cool camping is also about congregating around the campfire to share stories, sing songs, cook supper, toast marshmallows, or to simply enjoy the hypnotic effect of staring into the flames.

I didn't always think like this; the first time I went camping I lasted precisely two-and-a-half hours before booking into the nearest hotel. I wrote the whole thing off as a hideous, never-to-be-repeated experience and refused even to think about it.

Then one evening at dinner the conversation turned to camping and, listening to the stories around the table, I realised that the reason I hated camping was because I had been doing it all wrong.

Used to my creature comforts, I had imagined that camping should be an experience of deprivation and that – a little like an

endurance test – it was something one simply, well, endured. The thrill of camping, I'd thought, was in living to tell the tale. A few months later I decided to try again. This time, though, I aimed to make it a luxury experience and set about truly thinking of my tent as a home from home.

Rather than settling for a standard, modern nylon model, I chose a tipi instead. From the moment I stepped inside, the experience was completely different. A compulsive nester at home, I made sure that I had lots of comforting things with me and sleeping in my tent this time was a truly magical experience. There are, of course, many different types of camping and many different reasons for doing it. Maybe you're so in love that the idea of the two of you being entirely cut off from the word in a field all alone under the stars is the motivation that will fuel your trip.

Perhaps you and a crowd of friends are looking for a cheap fun break, or maybe you have small children and can't face the idea of a long-haul flight and a stuffy hotel, or are off to a festival. Whatever the reason, you couldn't have picked a better time as camping's never been so cool.

Camping is a brilliant way to recharge your batteries and escape from modern life. It's a back-to-nature experience that allows you to forget about the phone and email, to be utterly free to do what you want and to enjoy the elements. One of the real thrills of camping is the act of setting up camp itself. Of making your space beautiful and taking some time off from your life. It should be an experience that appeals to all your senses and one that makes you feel truly alive. When you're camping, you tend to spend a lot of time thinking about what you're going to eat and drink next. What the weather's going to do and how you'd never noticed before how dark it really is at night.

What you don't do is worry about real life and that, I suppose, is one of the real joys of camping. It allows you to experience things you haven't since childhood. The day stretches before you in a way that's unusual even on other kinds of holidays.

For children, camping is sheer bliss. In a world in which they're forced to grow up far too quickly, camping holidays offer them an utterly childlike adventure. And, like many grown-ups, they love the kit associated with camping.

There are so many different adventures to be had. From doing it alone – in a one-man hike tent, somewhere utterly remote – to camping in a tipi field full of people, each one is different. But the thrill of spending nights outside is the same however you do it.

This book is not designed to be an instruction manual; it's more a celebration of the art of camping. After all, sleeping outdoors under canvas is one of the few truly childish pleasures afforded to grown-ups and it's not often that one gets to play 'house' any more.

Camping is a brilliant way to recharge your batteries and escape from modern life... forget about the phone and email, to be utterly free to do what you want and to enjoy the elements

14 tents 18 tipis 22 yurts

essentials

Having the right kit is vitally important to your camping trip. Without it you might be cold, miserable and, perhaps worst of all, the least stylish in the field. So, don't leave home without planning ahead and deciding exactly what you need to take.

loitering within tent

Technology and design have moved on massively and leaky, cold tents are a thing of the past. Tents are now pretty cool places in which to hang out.

Tents come in all shapes and sizes, from the very small and inexpensive to luxury versions with multiple bedrooms and space for everything, including the kitchen sink. Tents offer a compact and cost-effective means of camping. It's important, though, that you choose a tent that best serves your needs and that you put it up properly. The weather can change really quickly and you need to ensure your tent offers you proper protection and will withstand the elements.

With tents, as with many things in life, you get what you pay for. Having said that, it makes no sense to spend a fortune on a tent if you're not sure if you're going to like camping. Larger camping shops have a good selection and staff who will be able to advise on the right tent for you. Whichever tent you go for, it's a good idea to practice putting it up at home before you take it away for the first time. Manufacturers'

instructions can be a bit of a nightmare to follow and forget about trying to put it up for the first time on site and in the dark or bad weather.

Second-hand tents can be a good idea if you're on a tight budget or are unsure if you'll enjoy camping. Local papers, eBay and army surplus stores are good places to hunt out bargains. If you can get hold of an old-fashioned Scouts or army tent made from proper canvas, then you'll have loads of space.

When you get to a temporary oasis, choose where you think you want to pitch your tent and sit on the grass for ten minutes. This is a useful exercise as it ensures it is indeed a good place to camp. Lie on the grass, too, and make sure it's flat, even and comfortable.

The next step is to pitch your tent. If you're a girl alone, you can always stand there batting your eyelashes and allow a knight in shining armour to do it for you. Whatever your tent

looks like on the outside, you can make it gorgeous on the inside.

The most important thing is comfort. As soon as your tent is pitched, decide what is going to go where and keep it meticulously tidy. If everything's in its place, you won't end up trying to find your torch in the pitch black or rolling over to find yourself putting your head on a pile of plates.

It's best to decide where your bed is going to be positioned first. I can cope with anything as long as I have a good night's sleep. But, if deprived of my full eight hours, even in the wilderness, I become impossible. Make sure you think about which way you want to face while sleeping. I like to have my feet facing the door, although at festivals it's quite popular to sleep with your head close to the door, so you can chat to your neighbours. Make your bed and pile on the pillows.

Next, choose your kitchen area, somewhere for clothes and somewhere for the important things including the torch, matches and corkscrew, books and chocolate. I think this is important regardless of the size of the tent.

Luxuries are an important part of tent life. Rugs are a must, for me at least. They can be heavy, though, so tricky if you're hiking. Groundsheets have a horribly crackly, utilitarian feel and walking on rugs is much more comfortable. They also help to keep the tent warm at night.

It's also vital to get the lighting right. Bright fluorescent torches are OK for walking to the loo at night, but in your tent you'll want an altogether softer light. Gas lamps are good for this, as are the lanterns that take tea-lights, but obviously take care to avoid any fire hazards.

Most campsites allow you to have a sleeping tent and a pup tent on your pitch. These are usually very small tents, but can be useful for storage.

If you're going camping with older children, they tend to love sleeping in their own tents. As long as it's safe I think this should be strongly encouraged. It makes it more of an adventure for them and more peaceful for you.

tent tips

Buy the best you can
Buy the best tent you can afford and never buy a tent without first having seen it up.

Hot advice...
If you're camping somewhere you're likely to get chilly, then line the base of your tent with a metallic safety blanket. Shiny side up, it'll reflect your body heat back into the tent.

Look for funky colours
Tents are often made in rather uninspiring colours, but you can hunt out some pretty ones. Cath Kidston makes gorgeous patterned ones for Millets.

The joy of text
If you're camping at a large campsite or festival, it's a good idea to put a flag on your tent. Orange developed a tent that lit up when you sent it a text message. Sadly, so far no one has made it commercially.

Make it your own
If you want to customise your tent make sure you do it safely. Paint and hangings can damage the waterproofing. A helium balloon flying from the top is always rather sweet, as is bunting.

Be prepared
Check the weight of the tent before you buy it. If you're travelling by car and can park right next to your pitch it's not an issue. If you're hiking up a large hill it most definitely is.

Keep bedding dry
Store your bedding in a bin bag to ensure that it doesn't get wet when you're making camp. There are few things as depressing as being out all day only to find yourself sleeping in a soggy bed when it's time to turn in.

tent types

Frame
These are the most like a house. They're large and you can walk around freely as there's enough headroom. Usually they have a number of separate rooms.

Vis-a-vis ❶
This means the tent has a bedroom at each side of the living area.

Pyramid ❷
These are triangular in shape and are easy to erect because they have a central pole.

Ridge
Traditional triangular tents, which are sturdy and offer a lot of headroom. Their weakness is that the sides are unsupported.

Lightweight/dome
The most suitable tents for backpackers as they're compact and aren't heavy. Dome tents come in larger sizes for families or those who want to camp in a crowd.

Geodesic ❸
These tents are similar to the dome variety, but because they have a different pole configuration they're sturdier in high winds.

Hoop ❹
These are like a cross between a ridge tent and a dome tent. They're lightweight, spacious and are good in windy conditions.

Inflatables
An ingenious invention, as you don't have to go through the palaver of erecting the tent, you simply blow it up with a foot pump.

tipiornottipi?

Everyone should sleep in a tipi at least once. Their combination of elegance and practicality, and the way they allow one to gaze at the stars at night, make them truly romantic and my favourite camping structure.

The magic of sleeping in a tipi is almost indescribable. Watching the stars through the open smoke flaps, while lying next to a roaring fire, is a wonderful experience. The tipi is probably the most elegant and graceful of all temporary structures and its beauty lies in its simplicity.

Phil Royle, from tipi.co.uk, who made my tipi, sums it up brilliantly. "Take twelve sticks, tie them together, wrap the canvas around, secure with more sticks and hang the lining. This is the recipe for a wonderful living space.

"Tipis are cool in the summer and in the winter, all you need to do is light a fire and you'll be perfectly cosy."

Tipis are available in various sizes. Mine is 16ft in diameter and sleeps six adults comfortably. One of the joys of a tipi is that it's made from proper canvas, so smells delicious when new. It also takes on the gorgeous scent of wood smoke.

Most tipis are made from canvas that is waterproof and rot-proof. You can also usually pay extra to have your canvas fire-proofed as well.

How you floor your tipi is a matter of choice. Many like the natural look, but others prefer coir matting or tons of rugs over a plastic groundsheet. I like to do half-and-half and have the back of the tipi (where we sleep) covered and the front (where we eat, play games and generally hang out) left bare.

Tipis offer a flexible space that you can easily style to reflect your personality. This applies to the outside, too. Many tipi makers offer colour canvas options. My tipi is mainly white, but has

essentials tipis

pink smoke flaps, which look lovely.

One of the great advantages of a tipi, is that you can have a fire in it. If you don't want to light one directly on the ground, you can have a wood-burning stove, a fire bowl or a cast-iron chiminea. Drifting off to sleep in a tipi, while the fire crackles, is an intensely relaxing experience.

The shape of the tipi, as well as being practical, has spiritual significance. According to Greg Bramford, from The Tipi Company, "traditionally the tipi was a temple as well as a home. The floor of the tipi represented the earth on which we live, the walls the sky, and the poles the trails from earth to the spirit world, the links between man and the great mystery".

There are a number of places where you can go and camp in a tipi. Many are included in the listings section. Also, there are companies who hire out tipis and will erect them at a site of your choosing. This can be a campsite, field or festival.

"I used to hire tipis for guests to sleep in when I had parties in the countryside," says designer Alice Temperley. "Then, a few years ago, I broke my shoulder rather badly and was bed-bound for a couple of months. When I was allowed to get up, my husband walked me to the orchard and he had bought me a tipi with coloured ribbons hanging from the poles. It is the most romantic gift I have ever had.

"In the summer, I sleep in my tipi whenever I go home to Somerset for the weekend. I have a big Balinese bed in there and lots of sheepskin, so it's a little luxury countryside retreat.

"I love tipis because they are just so special. Romantic and spacious and whenever I sleep in one I feel as if I'm not in the English countryside, but some magical place somewhere that cannot be explained, really."

Glastonbury festival's Emily Eavis says: "I love tipis. A tipi is the most beautiful place to camp. There are always lots of tipis at Glastonbury. They're all over the site and then there's the tipi field. It's amazing. They look really beautiful against the skyline."

Tipi tips

Fire safety
Remember to take a small fire extinguisher and a sharp knife in case you need to get out of the tipi quickly and your exit is blocked. Both of these should be hung from a string attached to one of the tipi poles and should be clearly visible.

Looking good
You can make your tipi look fantastic by hanging strings of beads from the poles inside, using fur throws and lots of cushions. Ribbons tied right at the end of the poles look great blowing in the wind.

Stay cool
The smoke flaps of your tipi act like a natural chimney and should, of course, be open whenever you have a fire inside the tipi. In the summer, though, they can also help create a through-draught which will keep the interior comfortably cool in warmer weather.

getting it up

The alternative guide to erecting a tipi

1. Stand there looking perplexed
You'll attract a crowd eager to advise

2. Chat for a bit
You'll make friends to join you in the tipi

3. Suggest opening a bottle
A glass of wine will pull things into focus

4. Get out paper and a pen
Draw a picture of how the tipi should look

5. Phone a friend for advice
Gossip and let them talk to your new friends

6. Elect a leader
They'll lose face if it all goes horribly wrong

7. Check the local hotel guide
Suddenly the great indoors is looking very attractive

everybody yurts

Hired by Madonna for her parties and bought by many people as second homes, yurts are simply gorgeous.

Out of all camping structures the yurt is perhaps the most flexible. They're surprisingly portable and easy to put up, but are robust enough to stay up for long periods. In Mongolia, the word for yurt (which is actually Russian) is 'ger' and it means 'home'.

The yurt is self-supporting. The frame is made from individual sections of wooden lattice work and the cover is made from canvas, felt or skins. The roof ring is the most complex element of the yurt. It's into this ring that the roof poles slot.

Nigel Harvey, a passionate camper who left school to become a shepherd in South America, knows a thing or two about camping. He runs a brilliant company called Ride World Wide, which arranges holidays on horseback all around the globe. The company uses Yurts in Mongolia and Nigel loves them. "I love the family life that goes on inside a yurt," he says. "And there's a lot of interest in the way they're put up. You have to lift the ring with sticks and prop it up. It's actually quite a mechanical feat.

"The yurt is amazingly intricate and has walls which keep in the warmth and a ventilation system which is little more than a cloth on a pole. It works really well though."

While arguably the coolest thing to camp in, the yurt is actually practical and, importantly, comfortable. If you're tall you don't get the same sense of being cramped in a yurt that you do in an ordinary tent.

The yurt is also one of the most proven of camping structures. Jonathan Morriss, of Bruton Yurts, agrees. "The design of the yurt as it is used in Mongolia today, has been proven over many years of use in a harsh and unyielding climate.

"The physical characteristics of these simple dwellings – strength, portability, and ease of

*my way

Martin Miller has some practical advice on under-canvas living

Martin Miller, described by A A Gill as 'beyond fashion' and the owner of Notting Hill's favourite rooming house, Miller's Residence, can't camp without...

Antimate to stop stray dogs peeing on your tent

Clear box so you can take the spider that's bitten you to the hospital with you

Proper chess set with fold-out legs

Hotel 'Do not disturb' sign

Large gong to call everyone to dinner

Persian carpet to add a sense of luxury

Outside tree candelabra

Compact PIR alarm

Green & Black's chocolate for breakfast

'Summer' by Summer Watson and some wake-up music, perhaps a CD of trumpet sonatas and a classic selection of military trumpet

erection – make them ideal practical structures for the 21st century nomad.

"However it is the feeling invoked by their internal space and structural beauty that alters the tempo of our lives. The relaxed and tranquil atmosphere somehow helps one to refocus, strengthened by the reassuring sense of history and tradition."

Television presenter Kevin McCloud is another yurt fan. "I love yurts; I harbour an ambition to travel the world and see how people build their homes.

"I think the noblest of all is the yurt. I like the fact I can stand up and walk all the way round. I spent two days in a yurt with a wood-burning stove and loved it."

Yurt tip
The shape of the yurt lends itself to serious interior design, allowing you to truly stamp your mark on it. This yurt and the one on the previous page, both of which are at Canvas Chic in France, are good examples of how amazing they can be.

stayingpower

If you don't fancy life under canvas, there are plenty of other options, each with its own unique blend of charm. There are so many funky bolt-holes available that one of the only problems is deciding which one to go for.

Taking to the road in a Romany caravan pulled along by a horse offers you a holiday that's the antithesis of modern life. The inevitable slow pace is hypnotic and you'll notice things you never have before. They're cosy at night, but airy during the day as the doors open wide.

Shepherds' huts are so sweet and can be surprisingly well equipped. Often they have wood-burning stoves, proper beds and carpets. A shepherd's hut in the middle of nowhere is brilliant for couples who are desperately in love and want isolation and privacy.

This is true of beach huts, too, and you have the added luxury of waking up to the sound of the waves rolling in.

If you want something super-cool, then look no further than an Airstream trailer. Lots of movie stars request them on set; Sean Penn lived in one, and you can even buy an Airstream with a Ralph Lauren-designed interior.

A campervan or caravan is brilliant for those who are easily bored in one place. They're also good if you fancy getting creative with your space, as you can stamp your own style on the interior. I think they look particularly sweet if you go for high kitsch when kitting them out.

A word of warning, though: it may well be a peculiarly British thing, but I'm always bemused by people who take to the road for an adventure and end up sitting in a lay-by on the side of the motorway, having their lunch or a cup of tea.

Instead, if you need a break, meander through country lanes and stop in beautiful country parks, woods, at a designated beauty spot, or on the outskirts of a pretty village.

metal gurus and bohemian bolt-holes

Caravan of love
This Romany caravan was built at the turn of the century for a Cornish circus dwarf, so is actually incredibly small. The colours and detail on these caravans are always stunning.

Beach hut breaks
These are great spaces to camp in and can be bought or hired at many beaches and now at festivals too. Tardis-like, they are far more spacious than you might think.

Camper crazy
The retro chic of a campervan is undeniable and second-hand ones are widely available. The original colours are gorgeous, but you can have them re-sprayed in any shade you like.

Shepherd's delight
Shepherds' huts are rather like Wendy houses for grown-ups. They're spacious and cosy and are brilliant to have in the garden as an extra room or somewhere to escape too.

T@b light
The T@b caravan is ridiculously sweet and, for something so small, unbelievably well equipped. Plus, they've done the seemingly impossible in making caravaning cool again.

Pod casts
A great way to hang out at festivals. The PodPad is sweet, functional, warm and will keep you dry in even the wettest of festival weather.

Air apparent
Vintage Airstreams are almost too cool. Spacious inside and stunning on the outside, they provide the ultimate environment in which to play house.

Hangin' around
It's great to sleep on a hammock swinging between two trees. If you prefer something a little sturdier, you can get hammocks with frames. There are versions to suit every budget.

27

you'llneedthese

How to make sure you don't spend the first night of your trip driving round looking for a late-night supermarket where you can buy matches and a torch.

I t's not for nothing that the scouts' motto is Be Prepared. If you're ill-prepared you're setting yourself up for a miserable trip. Cameron McNeish, editor of TGO (The Great Outdoors) magazine, and president of the Backpackers' Club, likes to camp alone and 'any place wild' and he makes preparedness an art form. The list of things he takes camping is so pared down compared to mine that it's almost funny.

His must-haves are as follows: tent, sleeping bag, stove, insulated pad, head torch, bottle to pee in at night, rucksack, food, water, insect repellent and a little whiskey to get through the night. Compare these to my own essentials of cushions, rugs, candles, books and other paraphernalia.

Cameron's most important piece of advice is this: "Never skimp on the sleeping bag. Invest in

a good one or you'll regret it." He also emphasises the importance of a hat. When your mother told you that you lose most of your body heat through your head she wasn't joking.

Though Cameron's brand of camping isn't for everyone (this is, after all, a man who takes dehydrated spaghetti bolognaise on his trips) it is truly inspiring and I'm rather envious of the complete sense of freedom he must feel camping alone on a mountain. When he explains why, it makes me think that one day I'll try it. "I enjoy being close to the earth," he says, "and mountains make me happy."

While you'll probably be camping somewhere a little less out of the way than the places Cameron favours, the rules about being prepared are just as important. It is, of course, not nearly as risky if you're unprepared in The Cotswolds, but you'll still have a miserable time if you get

Think pink
This gorgeous Swiss army knife
proves even essentials can
be stylish

Light fantastic
A good torch is a
must-take. This one is
lightweight and robust

Snug as a bug
I'm not a huge fan
of sleeping bags, but
if you use one make
sure it's well made

Bags of scope
You don't necessarily need a
huge back pack; instead try
something practical and stylish
like this Messenger bag

Spark of genius
This ingenious flint allows you to
start a fire without matches

essentials kit

Pretty in pink
A storm lamp is a surprisingly glamorous addition to your kitbag

Use your head
A headtorch is great for reading in bed or finding lost boots in the dark

"I'm in the tent"
A mobile phone is good for emergencies, but keep it switched off unless you need to use it

Firestarter
A windproof lighter is brilliant; just make sure it's topped up and the flint is new

drenched in the middle of the night and have no way of getting warm and dry again.

Choosing what to take and packing it all up is fun and is something you should take your time over.

Deciding what I'm going to wear, which luxuries cannot be left behind and what music to take, is a process that takes me at least two days. But then I take a lot.

Kit tip
You can buy solar-powered backpacks which allow you to charge equipment such as mobile phones, iPods, cameras, radios and other small electrical items. See Listings for more information.

Comfort blanket
You'll stay warm and stylish with blankets like these gorgeous mohair ones

hotadvice

TV presenter Kevin McCloud on the essential art of keeping warm

Clothing Spend your money on silk and cashmere and Botany wool. If you spend your money on yourself you'll be warmer and much more comfortable

Boots Get a pair of Brasher boots – they're lightweight and Gore-Tex lined, so are waterproof

Jackets Go for a Gore-Tex Pac-Lite jacket. They roll up to nothing and are breathable and waterproof. Also you need Pac-Lite trousers

Hats Tibetan cashmere woollen hat

Underwear I don't wear man-made fibres to keep warm. Instead I have cashmere socks and silk long-Johns (the silk wicks away moisture) and silk vests

Sweaters Next, I wear Botany thin wool or cashmere pullovers and finally the Gore-Tex layer on top

Camping philosophy It's all about keeping warm. The army motto is: "Any stupid * * * *er can get cold!"

essentials kit

Tea's made
A good kettle means
you'll always be able
to have a cuppa on
demand

Old flame
It's really important to have
the right sort of light when
you're camping. Try to make
sure it's not too harsh
or artificial

Cutting edge
A sharp knife
is a vital camp
kitchen tool

Pots and pans
Camp cookware can
suffer on the fire, so
make sure yours is sturdy
and doesn't have wood
or plastic handles

If, like me, you have a favourite pan for each dish you cook and a selection of knives that would put a circus act to shame, then you'll have to resign yourself to paring down a bit when it comes to your camp kitchen. I don't, however, subscribe to the camping philosophy that says everything you take camping should be cheap and almost disposable. There is no good reason why you can't take some of your favourite equipment from your kitchen with you as long as you're prepared for what might happen to it if you use it on a campfire.

While I have china and glass set aside purely for camping, it lives in a wicker hamper in my pantry and is always ready to go, I don't have pots, pans, knives or any other equipment specially for camping. Silly as it would sound to non-cooks, you build a relationship with your kitchen equipment and I see no reason why you should be unfaithful to it just because you're away from home. Obviously, that doesn't mean you have to take all of it.

To a degree, camp cooking is about planning ahead, but it's also about improvisation. Take a

large roll of heavy duty foil with you and you'll be able to find your way around most cooking hiccups. Great cooks are intuitive and, like good workmen, never blame their tools or lack of them. It's actually rather easy to become the sort of cook who can seemingly rustle up fabulous food from nothing. It's all about keeping things simple, not trying too hard, and editing your equipment needs.

While at home it's nice to have something for every kitchen task, in the great outdoors it's quite refreshing to have to make do. I think it makes you more creative in the way you cook and allows you to cook things you perhaps wouldn't at home.

Barbecues are brilliant for camping. Bucket-shaped barbecues are brilliant and disposable barbecues are good if you have a space issue.

Of course, cooking over an open fire is the ultimate in camp cuisine. I've never tried this one myself, but my editor reliably informs me that if you buy a new metal dustbin, turn it on its side and lay it in your campfire coals and replace the lid you will have a DIY oven perfect for baking brownies or roasting

Milking it
A milk churn is surprisingly useful when camping. You can, for example, fill it with water and keep it by the fire just in case it gets out of control

Pail and interesting
This ingenious barbecue looks as good as it cooks

a whole chicken. One also shouldn't forget camp stoves. They allow you to control the temperature and mean you don't have to collect wood for the fire. However, don't forget to take enough Propane for elaborate meals or long stays.

Cast-iron frying pans are useful when camping, but are also quite heavy so not for those who are walking or determined to travel light. A fish slice and tongs are essential as often you cook over a very high heat when camping. And it's essential not to forget things like oven gloves and pot grabs. Pans are no cooler because you're outdoors and you need to be careful you don't burn yourself when cooking.

Think, too, about the small things that'll make supper much nicer. These include salt and pepper mills – so you don't end up using those hideous sachets – napkins and decent olive oil.

It's actually liberating to cook with a limited range of equipment. Eating is a different matter. Unless you're travelling light, it's nice to take lovely china and glass if you can. Personally, I hate with a passion drinking from plastic or using plastic cutlery. It seems somehow to taint the food.

Basket cases
Useful for both full and
empty bottles

Cool it!
A good cool bag is an absolute
essential for camping. At many campsites,
there's a place where you can re-freeze
your ice packs

Glove affair
Gorgeous, warm and
seriously chic

Head start
Don't forget
to keep your
head warm
and dry

It's a wrap!
A scarf will
keep you cosy
and stylish

Pyjama game
Don't wear a
faded t-shirt
in bed. Instead
wear gorgeous
PJs like these

**Best foot
forward**
Proof that
wellies come in
colours other
than green

essentials

Warm colours
The best way to
keep warm and
stay stylish is
to layer

On your wavelength
Funky radios are so
gorgeous and perfect if
you can't bear to miss your
favourite programmes

The vinyl cut
Even in the
great outdoors
you can enjoy
favourite albums

Don't fret
No campfire gathering is complete
without a guitar god and a seriously
gorgeous acoustic

37

40 etiquette 46 fires

out there

There are so many elements that go into making a camping trip fun and each of them is important in its own way. Being prepared and knowing what to expect makes a trip infinitely more enjoyable.

48 stories   52 songs   54 games

goodneighbours

No one can be truly stylish unless they have exquisite manners. Camping is a form of communal living and gives you the perfect opportunity to show off yours.

Good manners are back in fashion and, in many ways, it's actually more important to be exquisitely polite when you're living in the great outdoors than it is when you're between four walls. It's important to respect nature, the environment and others. For example, never go into someone's tent without being invited. Of course, you can't knock on the door, but a simple hello should alert them to your presence.

The issue of noise is a difficult one as there are most definitely two sides to every volume dispute. I think the best thing to do is find out about the noise policy of places you're considering camping at and find one that suits you best. If you have small children it can be infuriating to have a raucous party going on next to you when you're trying to get them to sleep. Equally, if you're camping with a crowd of friends you won't appreciate the noise police pitching up – tutting – at 9pm on the dot.

Although camping is romantic and canoodling under canvas, or even under the stars, can be blissful, you do have to be considerate to those near you. A friend of mine found herself having to explain the birds and bees prematurely to her four-year-old son, at three in the morning in the middle of a field, as they endured a rather noisy performance from the couple in the next tent.

out there etiquette

I've never camped without borrowing from or lending something to my fellow campers. From torches to corkscrews, there's always something someone's forgotten. It can be rather charming to take a pack of note cards with you to jot down a quick thank you before you leave.

Camping with kids has its own set of rules. Make sure that no one set of parents ends up looking after a whole crowd of children. Also ensure that your children never outstay their welcome in someone else's tent. Plus, it's a good idea to have extra treats for visiting kids.

If you're camping somewhere that allows pets, you need to be a responsible owner. I know from experience how utterly infuriating it is to have a dog pee on your tent. Unless you have a 'world's best-behaved dog' rosette hanging on your wall then keeping your dog on a lead will lessen the risk of embarrassment. Also, it's important to always clean up after your dog.

Finally, don't burn anything other than paper or wood on the campfire as it'll smell horrible and leave a mess. It's also bad for the environment.

Serenity is an important aspect of camping, so make sure you don't spoil it for others. Make your space your own, of course, but be aware of how it may impact on those around you.

likewewereneverhere

Get to know the Leave No Trace principles of camping.

Plan ahead and prepare

Know the regulations and special concerns of the area. Prepare for extreme weather, hazards, and emergencies. Schedule your trip to avoid times of high use. Visit in small groups or split larger parties into groups of 4-6. Repackage food to minimise waste. Use a map and compass to eliminate the use of marking paint, rock cairns or flagging.

Travel and camp on durable surfaces

Durable surfaces include established trails and campsites, rock, gravel, dry grasses or snow. Protect riparian areas by camping at least 200ft from lakes and streams. Good campsites are found, not made. Altering a site is not necessary. In popular areas, concentrate use on existing trails and campsites, walk in single file in the middle of the trail, even when wet or muddy, keep campsites small and focus activity in areas where vegetation is absent. In pristine areas, disperse use to prevent the creation of campsites and trails. Avoid places where impacts are just beginning.

Dispose of waste properly

Pack it in, pack it out. Inspect your campsite and rest areas for trash or spilled foods. Deposit solid human waste in catholes dug 6-8 inches deep and at least 200 feet from water, camp and trails. Cover and disguise the cathole when finished. Pack out toilet paper and hygiene products. To wash yourself or your dishes, carry water 200ft away from streams or lakes and use small amounts of biodegradable soap. Scatter strained dishwater.

Leave what you find

Preserve the past: examine, but do not touch, cultural or historic structures and artifacts. Leave rocks, plants and other natural objects as you find them. Avoid introducing or transporting non-native species. Do not build structures, furniture, or dig trenches.

Minimise campfire impacts

Campfires can cause lasting impacts. Use a lightweight stove for cooking and a candle lantern for light. Where fires are permitted, use established fire rings, fire pans, or mound fires. Keep fires small. Only use sticks from the ground that can be broken by hand. Burn all wood and coals to ash, put out campfires completely, then scatter cool ashes.

Respect wildlife

Observe wildlife from a distance. Do not follow or approach animals. Never feed them. Protect wildlife and your food by storing rations and trash securely. Control pets. Avoid wildlife at sensitive times: mating, nesting, raising young or in winter.

Be considerate of other visitors

Respect other visitors. Be courteous. Yield to other users on the trail. Take breaks and camp away from trails and other visitors. Let nature's sounds prevail. Avoid loud voices and noise.

Leave No Trace guidance courtesy of the Center for Outdoor Ethics

*fire*starter

Bluffer's guide to lighting a fire...

Unless you're survival expert Ray Mears or have been attending Brownie or Scout camp for the last 50 years, it's unlikely you'll be able to make a fire by rubbing two sticks together. Instead, try this method.

① Gather your firewood

You'll need three types – kindling, sticks and larger pieces of wood. It's important to make sure all the wood you use is fallen wood and is totally dry.

② Choose where to site your campfire

If there's a place where a fire has been lit before then use it. If not, choose somewhere sheltered, away from flammable items (including your tent!) and where no damage to flora or fauna will be done. Dig a shallow fire pit and make a ring of stones around it.

③ Getting the fire going

Arrange the kindling into a pyramid shape. Start with small pieces and work outwards, so larger pieces are on the outside. You can always scrunch up paper and put kindling on top. If you're desperate, you can also use a firelighter or two to help things get going, but never use lighter fuel or barbecue fluid on an open flame. Place a lit match on the kindling; it should catch fire and spread to the sticks and wood on top. You can gently blow around the base to get the kindling going, then add wood to keep it going.

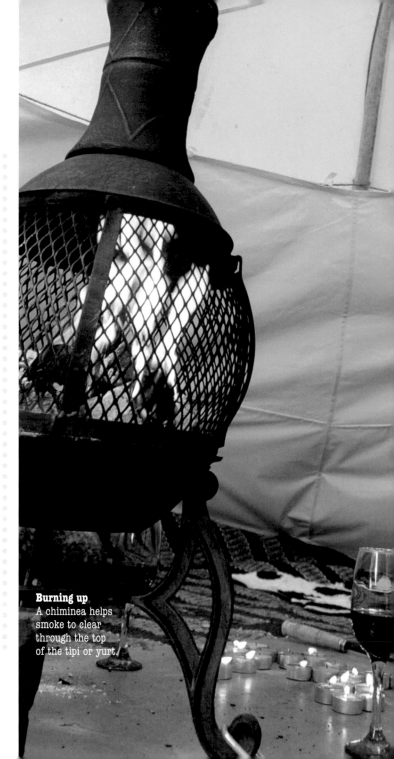

Burning up
A chiminea helps smoke to clear through the top of the tipi or yurt.

light my fire

The campfire is the focus that pulls everyone in and makes it a communal experience. It's where you cook, eat, chill out, sing songs, play games and generally stay warm. So knowing how to build a sustainable, safe fire is crucial.

I love campfires. Without them camping would be an infinitely less romantic experience. The sight, smell and sound of a campfire linger in the memory, instantly evocative. There's something elemental about sitting together around the only source of heat and, perhaps, the only means you have to cook. They're also surprisingly easy to build and keep going.

Chef Mitchell Tonks sums it up perfectly. "You need a campfire. It's the place where you eat, drink, play music and chew the fat. It's also where you play games, toast marshmallows, tell stories and generally hang out."

Campfires draw people in. If you're camping with a fire you're likely to make a lot of new friends – people can't resist coming over and warming up for a few minutes. This communal feel can make camping and campfires all the more enjoyable.

If you're camping in a tipi or yurt, you can have a fire inside, like the one pictured, which is truly amazing. One of the real joys of camping in a tipi is to gather round the fire while the rain pours down outside and you're cosy and warm.

Often campsites will have one large communal campfire, which is wonderful if you're the social type, as it's certainly where you'll find the crowd. It's also rather handy if you're new to campfire cooking as there'll be plenty of people to offer advice.

It pays to light your fire early, so it's not too dark and you're not too cold. If you leave it too late the temptation to go to bed, just to keep warm, will overwhelm you and you'll miss out on one of the great camping pleasures. Often you'll find there are organised events, such as fish nights or quizzes, round the fire. Some campsites also have an outdoor oven or grill, where you can cook your own food and perhaps even get to taste a little of other campers' culinary delights.

firesafety

Quick guide to safe campfires

Campfire safety is critically important, but by following a few simple rules you can enjoy your fire without having to worry.

How will you put it out?
Have a means of extinguishing the fire close by. This can be a bucket of water, a hose attached to a tap or a bucket full of sand. After all, you don't want to be responsible for a forest fire.

Mind the gap
Don't build your fire too close to tents, trees or anything else that could catch fire.

Stay around to supervise
Never leave your campfire unattended.

Small things matter
Pay close attention to children round the fire.

Burning issues
Never burn plastic, aerosol containers or anything that isn't wood or paper.

Abide by the rules
It's also important to check the campfire policy of your site. Some have a strict no-fire policy, while others allow fires only in designated areas. I couldn't bear to camp without a fire, so I always check the policy before I decide where I'm going to camp.

onedarknight

Camping wouldn't be the same without spooky stories around the campfire. Here are a few sure to scare.

Just why ghost stories and campfires go so well together I don't know. Perhaps it's being outside in the dark, or maybe it's the sound of the great outdoors, the owls screeching and the leaves rustling. Whatever it is that makes it so, ghost stories have long been a part of the camping experience.

Of course, you do have to be careful of terrifying small children, or those of a nervous disposition. It's also worth popping to the loo before the scary stuff starts, as you won't want to wander off alone mid-story.

Scouting websites have great stories, many of which have instructions on how to act them out, which can be great fun for a younger audience. Props, too, can be fun. Try giving children leaves to rustle or keys to jangle, anything that adds to the story and makes them feel part of it.

It's also worth picking up a book of classic Victorian or Edwardian ghost stories as they can be seriously spooky. Of course, it's not just

stories; poetry works well too.

Emma Bridgewater agrees: "We have a good friend who's amazing to camp with, because he knows hundreds of poems off by heart. Some of them are really spooky."

It can actually be surprisingly romantic telling ghost stories around the fire as we all want to snuggle up when we're scared. Dating experts recommend horror movies for the same reasons.

The best thing about stories is that everyone can join in. It's rare to find someone who hasn't had a spooky encounter, or at least been told of one by a friend.

Simply talking about the time a door opened of its own accord for no apparent reason, or remembering an occasion when the temperature in a room inexplicably dropped, can be enough to put you in the mood.

out there stories

Room for one more inside

A man spent the night with some friends in their old country house. They had a lovely evening and all staggered off to bed rather late. In the middle of the night the man was woken by what sounded like horses hooves on cobble-stones outside. He sat up in bed to listen more closely and heard what sounded like people getting into a carriage.

There was lots of chatter and the only thing he could make out clearly was the driver saying loudly, 'room for one more inside'. The next morning he went down for breakfast and told his hosts what he'd heard and asked why they had a horse-drawn carriage outside so late at night.

At first they were surprised and confused, but they quickly became amused and told him he must have dreamed it or had one too many drinks at dinner.

Years passed and the man forgot all about the strange incident. He then travelled to India and was in the lobby of a very grand hotel. Making his way across the hall he reached the crowded lift and was about to get in when he heard exactly the same voice as he had all those years ago. It said 'room for one more inside'.

The hairs on the back of his neck stood up and he quickly turned away from the lift. The lift door had closed by the time he turned back just in time to hear it plummet downwards with the people trapped inside. They all died.

The mysterious hitch-hiker

A young man has been out for the night with friends. He drives around, dropping them off, until the last one has gone and he is alone. After driving for a few minutes he sees a girl standing by the side of the otherwise deserted country road. She's holding out her thumb for a lift.

He stops and opens the door for her. She gets in and he's staggered by how beautiful she is. They chat about trivial things and he notices she is shivering. He offers her his jacket.

Deciding he's going to ask her out, he walks round the car to open her door, but he's too late. She's nowhere to be seen. He figures she got a little nervous and ran into the house.

The next day he realises she still has his jacket and is thrilled he has an excuse to see her again. He goes to her house and an older woman who looks a lot like her answers the door. He explains what happened and the woman looks at him oddly. She goes into the house and comes out with a photograph.

'Is this the girl you picked up?' she asks. He confirms it is. The woman says she has something to show him and takes him out of the house to the churchyard just down the road. As they walk, she explains her daughter had been killed in a car crash at the spot where he says he picked her up. As they approach her grave he can see something hanging from it. It isn't long before they both realise it's his jacket.

ging gang goolie...

Open the marshmallows, tune the guitar and practice your scales because this is where the joy of camping hots up.

Part of the fun of camping is making your own entertainment. Nowadays we're rather spoiled by a 24-hour culture in which there's always something diverting available. Camping allows for a more traditional approach.

Games around the fire work well for all age groups and can be as silly or competitive as the group likes. I like a mix of songs and games and prefer to play things that don't go on for hours. If you're playing a game where people go 'out' when they lose, it can be a bit dull for them while everyone else plays on. So try to choose fast-paced games that allow everyone a turn in the spotlight. There are some game ideas on page 54 to get you going.

Music, for me at least, is essential. The idea of camping without it feels a little soulless. Whether it's music to listen to in the tent or songs sung or played around the campfire, without music the experience is compromised.

Of course you can belt out campfire favourites such as *Ging Gang Goolie* or *The Quartermaster's Store*, but you'll probably want something a little cooler. Beatles songs are always easy to sing along to and, as John Hannah said in *Sliding Doors*, we're all somehow born knowing the lyrics.

Good ones for the campfire are *Get By With a Little Help from My Friends*, *Here Comes the Sun* and *Yesterday*. If you're camping with children then *Yellow Submarine* always goes down well, they also rather enjoy re-working the lyrics to this one for some reason.

Everyone I've spoken to seems to agree that camping requires a soundtrack filled with Van Morrison and Bob Dylan. *Brown-Eyed Girl* is always a crowd pleaser and *Spanish Rose* just sounds like summer. *Moondance* is one of my all-time favourite tracks and is pretty good for

**Alex James
on his favourite
campfire tracks**

There's a really good book called 101 Hits for Buskers. So I recommend you pop to Denmark Street in London before you go camping and buy one because it's got every song you'll need.

The Lion Sleeps Tonight is a great song. You can have one lot singing the top line, while the others sing the 'a wimowehs'. In fact, anything with two parts is good.

A family favourite of the James' is The Peanut Vendor, which is brilliant and you can make the words up as you go along.

California Dreamin's tricky, but when you pull it off it's brilliant.

Any man who's prepared to learn one Bee Gees song will be a great man around the campfire.

Percussion's good, so take a tambourine, kazoo or anything you can bang. Cavemen used to bang mammoth skulls together and then go off and have orgiastic sex around the campfire – a bit like a modern festival!

late-night romantic camping. Good Bob Dylan songs include *Tambourine Man*, *It Ain't Me Babe*, *Like a Rolling Stone* and *Catfish*. And Bob Marley's *Exodus* and *Jammin'* are made for the kind of late-night vibe you get round a fire.

For an altogether sunnier feel you might want to think about some Beach Boys songs. *Sloop John B* and *Wouldn't It Be Nice* are brilliant, particularly if you're camping by the sea.

As for games, there are so many you can try. Here, though, are a few to get you going. The most important thing is to have fun, so if it's getting dull move on and play something else.

Poker

Poker, as a game of bluff, can be even more challenging when you can't always 'read' people's faces in the dark. I rather like it when you play for something other than money. Perhaps the loser can be in charge of washing-up the next day, or the winner is allowed to sleep on while someone else looks after the children. Alternatively, the loser could be charged with cooking up a gastro camp feast.

The Eternal Story

The first person in the circle says a word such as 'I'. The second one may take up the story with the word 'went'. The third with 'to'. The fourth with 'the'. The fifth with 'woods'. And so on. The aim of the story is not to allow the sentence to finish. Players can make it difficult for each other by offering penultimate words that are difficult to continue from. The player who says the last word of a sentence is out and the game continues without him or her.

Game on
A wonderfully quirky and
chic take on outdoor life

Spot the Lie

This is a great game that allows you to find out fascinating facts about fellow campers. A member of the group must make three personal statements. Two of these must be true and the third one a lie. So, for example, they may say 'I went on a belly-dancing course. I can speak Swahili and I am a qualified pilot'. The group must decide which is a lie. This goes on until all have made their three statements.

21 Dares

You sit in a circle and one person starts counting from 'one'. You can say up to three numbers, for example 1, 2, and then the next person can say 3, 4, 5, etc. You carry on doing this until you get to 21. Whoever says 21 has to do a truth or dare dreamed up by the other members of the group. The object of the game is to not say 21, so change the amount of numbers you say on your turn to make sure you're not picked.

I Have Never...

This is a great game to play as a new couple. You'll find out all sorts of extraordinary things about each other. You can play it with jelly beans or as a drinking game. The first person makes a statement about something they've never done. For example, 'I have never been to New York'. If the second person has, they take a jelly bean or a drink and make their own 'I have never' statement.

Games tip

Board games are a brilliant idea on camping trips as they instantly take you back to childhood.

camp games

Designer Emma Bridgewater on camping fun

You must have a sing-along with a very groovy teenager and someone who knows all the words.

We've camped with Compo rations for true authenticity, but my husband Matthew found it wore thin rather quickly, as he likes to cook really delicious food when camping.

Never camp without a fire and always take some newspaper to help get it started.

Matthew found this brilliant thing at an ironmonger's in France. It's a sort of grill with a handle, four feet and a barred surface so you can put a kettle on it or cook on it.

My dad was a stalwart camper and always had a folding camp bed with proper sheets.

I have a blanket sleeping bag my grandmother made for my aunt for pony club.

I think my luxury would be a mattress, so I wouldn't have to have that haggle with myself over how many blankets I sleep on and how many I have for covers.

I hate sleeping in a nylon bubble. We had a 10 x10 canvas marquee. We'd hang a chandelier from the roof. We wore it out camping. In the end it just fell apart.

I can't camp without my husband, a bottle of wine, seaside location and a sharp knife.

campfire food

Indian Lamb Skewers Indian-spiced Lamburgers
Vegetable Bean Soup Sausages with Spicy Tomato
Lentils Scotch Broth Shellfish with Roasted Garlic
and Thyme Charred Prawns with Indian Spices
Grilled Marinated Red Mullet Marlin with Thyme
Leaf Herb-smoked Lobster Chicken and Prawn
Gumbo One-Pot Noodles Breakfast Fried Rice
Hot Chocolate Baked Banana Camp Treat Smores

moveablefeast

Repeat after me... 'I will not eat baked beans, and tinned meat is a crime against humanity. I can eat well in a tent.' Try these recipes to give your camp food the gastro edge.

Food somehow tastes better when you're camping. Even a humble bacon sandwich is transformed into something altogether more special. I think it's rather a shame to go to all the effort that camping entails and then simply to eat baked beans or other tinned food. Camping dishes should be simple and you should rely on the ingredients and method of cooking rather than any torturous preparation.

If at all possible catch or collect your own food (hedgehogs are not recommended). If you're camping somewhere with good fishing, then it would be a shame not to cook your own catch at least once. Do, though, check the local regulations.

One of the best things about cooking on a campfire is that it's always hot and ready, so if you're still hungry after supper you can make another pudding or put some hot chocolate on to keep out the evening chill.

It's nice to cook what's available locally. It adds to the experience and allows you to eat things you might not normally have. In the U.K at least, you're never far from a farm shop or farmers' market, so make the most of them.

You can cook on a barbecue, camp stove or campfire. For the recipes here that have longer cooking times, you'll need to ensure that you have a lot of propane if cooking on a stove. If a recipe needs a dish to simmer, then on a campfire you can move the pan closer to the outside edge of the fire where the heat will be less intense. On a camp stove, you can, of course, simply turn it down.

Tripods are useful for cooking over campfires, many of them designed so you can raise and lower your cooking pot, allowing you to have some degree of 'control' over the cooking temperature.

Hugh Fearnley-Whittingstall's recipes are always brilliant. These here, from 'The River Cottage Meat Book' (Hodder & Stoughton), are perfect if you're taking a barbecue on your camping trip. They're quick, easy and taste fantastic.

Indian-spiced Lamb Skewers

Lamb is the ultimate meat for barbecuing, its unmistakable flavour always shining through the smoky, chargrilled taste. You can use the same marinade for lamb chops. Serve with plain rice or naan bread, a good fruity chutney and a cooling raita made by mixing plain yoghurt with a little crushed garlic, diced cucumber, salt and pepper.

Ingredients
(Serves 6)
1kg boned-out shoulder or leg of lamb or mutton, trimmed and cut into 4cm cubes
1-4 small dried red chillies (depending on size and heat)
2 teaspoons coriander seeds
1 teaspoon fenugreek seeds
1 teaspoon mustard seeds
1 teaspoon black peppercorns
1 tablespoon olive or sunflower oil
3 garlic cloves, finely chopped
Salt

Method
Split the chillies open and remove and discard the seeds. Place in a pestle and mortar with the other dry spices and pound to a coarse powder.

Put the lamb in a bowl and mix with the oil and garlic, massaging it well so it is covered with a light film of oil. Toss thoroughly with the pounded spices and then leave to marinate for at least 2 hours.

Thread the meat on to 6 long skewers, soaked in water for 30 minutes first, if wooden. Lay them over a hot barbecue (or indoors on a ridged grill pan). Turn after a couple of minutes, then continue to turn regularly, seasoning with the odd sprinkling of salt. They'll take about 6-8 minutes to be cooked right through, but you can serve them a little pinker if you like.

Variation

Indian-spiced Lamburgers

Use the same quantities of seasonings for 1 kg minced lamb – but be cautious with the chillies (use $1/2$ teaspoon dried chilli flakes, if you like).

Form into patties 2 cm thick and barbecue (or fry) for 4-5 minutes on each side, till nicely browned and cooked through. Serve with the same accompaniments.

I can't think of anyone I'd rather have as the camp cook than my great friend, Lucy Young. This soup will keep out the cold. If you're cooking this on a campfire, then move the pan to the outer edge for the simmering phase as it will be cooler there.

Vegetable Bean Soup

Ingredients
(Serves 4-6)
1 medium leek, roughly chopped
1 stick celery, in 5mm dice
25g button mushrooms, sliced
1 x 400g can chopped tomatoes
900ml vegetable stock
1 x 400 g can butter beans, drained and rinsed
2 tbsp redcurrant jelly
1 tbsp sundried tomato paste
4 tbsp fresh breadcrumbs
Salt and pepper
Chopped fresh parsley
to garnish

Method
Tip the prepared leek, celery and mushrooms into a deep saucepan and pour in the chopped tomatoes and stock. Bring to the boil, cover and simmer for about 10 minutes. Add the rinsed beans, redcurrant jelly and tomato purée, and continue to simmer covered for a further 10-15 minutes, or until the vegetables are tender.

Add the breadcrumbs and season. Bring back to the boil over a high heat for a couple of minutes. Garnish with the parsley and serve with warm crusty bread.

campfire food

These recipes are from the inimitable Wilfred Emmanuel-Jones, who likes to be known as The Black Farmer. These are perfect for keeping out the cold. Make sure you keep the campfire going, as both will take a while to cook.

Sausages with Spicy Tomato Lentils

Ingredients
(Serves 6)
1 jar of tomato sauce
12 sausages, grilled
2 tbsp olive oil
2 onions, chopped
1 carrot, diced
3 cloves garlic, crushed and chopped
Large sprig of rosemary
300g puy lentils
850ml chicken stock
2 tbsp flat-leaf parsley, chopped

Method
Heat the oil in a large frying pan. Add the onions, carrots, garlic and rosemary. Cook gently, without browning, for 5-10 minutes until the onions are soft and translucent. Add the lentils, stock, tomato sauce and sausages. Season, bring to the boil then cover and simmer for about 40 minutes. Before serving stir in a handful of chopped flat leaf parsley. Serve with a green salad.

Scotch Broth

Ingredients
(Serves 6)
1.25kg middle neck lamb chops
85g pearl barley
2 tsp bouquet garni
Salt and freshly ground black pepper
3 medium carrots, diced
1 medium swede, diced
1 leek, washed well and chopped
2 tbsp parsley, chopped

Method
Trim any excess fat from the lamb bones and put in a large pot with the pearl barley and bouquet garni. Season well. If it's easier, you can do this at home before you leave. Pour in about 2 litres of water. Bring to the boil and allow to simmer for about an hour. Skim off any scum that rises to the surface. Add the carrot, swede and leek, adding more water if necessary. Return to the boil and simmer for another 30 minutes or until the vegetables are tender. Remove from the heat and fish the bones out of the pan. Take the meat off the bones and cut into small pieces; return to the pan. Scoop off any excess fat and check for seasoning. Ladle into bowls, sprinkle over the parsley and serve with crusty bread.

I've never eaten a fish better than one cooked by Mitchell Tonks. These recipes from 'The Aga Seafood Cookery Book' and 'FishWorks Seafood Café Cookbook' (Absolute Press) are utterly divine and are perfect for beach camping.

Shellfish with Roasted Garlic and Thyme

Ingredients

(Serves 3-4)
8 unpeeled large cloves of garlic
100ml olive oil
Salt
Splash of good white wine
Good handful of mussels
6 small raw shell-on prawns
3-4 langoustines
50g squid
Handful of clams
Handful of cooked bucatini
Pinch of chilli flakes, or 2 very tiny red hot, dried chillies
3-4 sprigs of thyme
Half a cup of home-made tomato sauce or passata (use the rustic chunky variety)

Method

Put the cloves of garlic with the olive oil onto the hot barbecue for a few minutes to roast them, then remove. Lay out a square of tin foil, large enough to hold all the ingredients and be folded and sealed tightly into a parcel. Turn up the sides and add a splash of wine, the garlic and the remaining ingredients, with the exception of the thyme and tomato sauce or passata. Toss it all together and place in a heap on the tin foil. Pour over the tomato sauce or passata and lay the thyme sprigs on top. Fold the tin foil up to make a tightly sealed parcel, cook on the barbecue for about 25 minutes.

Charred Prawns with Indian Spices

Mix some curry paste with yoghurt and then add fresh coriander. Split the prawns open down the back and marinate them in this mixture for an hour (and keep in a cool place). Put them on the barbecue for 6-7 minutes, depending on their size, turning occasionally. Finish with a squeeze of lime.

Grilled Marinated Red Mullet

Take some oregano, mix it with the juice of a lemon and a few tablespoons of olive oil and marinate the red mullet fillets in it for 5-10 minutes. Cook the fish in a hot pan on the campfire or straight on the barbecue for 4-5 minutes until crisp and golden. Serve with a green salad.

Marlin with Fresh Thyme Leaf and Lemon

Make a salsa rossa by mixing together a clove of garlic (chopped), 1 chopped, de-seeded red pepper, 2 shredded leaves of radicchio, a handful of chopped basil, a handful of chopped mint, 1 tsp of capers, 1 small deseeded chopped red chilli, 2 chopped anchovy fillets and a chopped tomato. Add lemon juice and sea salt to taste. Marinate a marlin steak in lemon zest, garlic and thyme leaf for 15 minutes. Grill either side for 3 minutes, squeeze on some lemon juice and serve.

Herb-smoked Lobster

Split a cooked lobster in half and remove the meat from the tail. Spread some garlic butter in the shell, sprinkle on a selection of chopped herbs and lay the meat back in. Put the lobster, shell side down, on the camp fire or barbecue and cover with an upside down casserole dish or similar. Place some bunches of rosemary and thyme on the charcoal and let the smoke go up inside the dish, which will take on a herby fragrance.

Tom Norrington-Davies is one of Britain's most exciting food writers. He has a column in the Weekend section of The Daily Telegraph where these recipes first appeared. Camping can be hungry work, but these are sure to keep you going.

Chicken and Prawn Gumbo

Something about this Cajun recipe feels like it was meant to be eaten round a campfire.

Real gumbo is thickened with okra but you could do a lot worse than to add some fresh sweet corn, shucked from the cob.

Ingredients
(Serves 4)
4 tbsp vegetable oil
2 cobs sweet corn
(or 6 tbs tinned sweetcorn)
3 breasts free range chicken boned and roughly diced
3 sticks celery
2 cloves garlic
1 leek, 1 green pepper, 1 onion, all finely chopped
1 bay leaf and a sprig of thyme
(optional)

1 level tsp plain flour
1 level tsp mild paprika
1 x 400g tin plum tomatoes, drained of all juices and squished
1 pint water
5 tsp Tabasco sauce
1 tsp Worcestershire or soy sauce
8oz cooked and peeled prawns
Salt to taste

Method
To shuck sweetcorn, stand the cob on its end in a bowl. Run a small knife down the length, shaving off the kernels as you go. Set aside.

Heat one tablespoon of the oil in a large pot and brown the chicken pieces in batches. Remove and set aside. Add the remaining oil and fry the celery, garlic, leek, pepper and onions, plus herbs. Cook them fairly briskly, for about ten minutes, stirring to stop them catching. Then sprinkle the flour and paprika over the vegetables and stir in.

Add the chicken, corn, tomatoes and the stock, then the Tabasco. Bring to a boil, then turn down the heat and simmer for about ten more minutes.

Finally, add the prawns and bring to a simmer for another five minutes or so. Check the seasoning and serve over rice.

One-Pot Noodles

Ingredients

(Serves 4)
1 tbsp vegetable oil
1 inch cube ginger, peeled, chopped
2 cloves garlic, peeled, chopped
125g oyster or field mushrooms, roughly sliced
1 onion, finely sliced
2 sticks celery, finely sliced
1 red pepper, finely sliced
1 courgette, cut into batons
1 tbsp ketchup
Juice of 1 lemon
2 tbsp soy sauce
1 tsp sugar (optional)
400ml water
Handful (125ml) peas
2 handfuls (125ml) dried egg noodles, roughly broken

Method

Heat the oil and fry the ginger and garlic until they are just starting to brown. Add the mushrooms and give them a 30-second head start over the onion, celery and pepper. Add together and fry for another minute before adding the ketchup, lemon juice, soy, sugar and water. When the mix starts to simmer, add the peas and the noodles and cook, stirring, until the liquid has become a glossy sauce and the noodles are tender.

Breakfast Fried Rice

Ingredients

(Serves 4)
4 eggs
2 tbsp vegetable oil
2 onions, chopped
2 or 3 thin strip rashers of bacon
2 handfuls peas (thawed if frozen)
4 handfuls cold, cooked rice
1 tbsp Worcestershire sauce
1 tbsp tomato ketchup
Half tsp salt

Method

Beat the eggs. Heat 1 tbsp of the oil in a wide pan or wok and when it is very hot add the eggs. Let the eggs begin to set like an omelette, then break them up with the end of a spoon and let them really overcook. Remove this dry 'scramble' and set it aside. Now return the pan to the heat, add the second tbsp of oil and fry the onions with the bacon, briskly. They will only need 2 or 3 minutes. Add the peas and stir fry for 1 minute. Add the rice and the seasonings then fry briskly again, until the rice is heated through. Finally, stir the eggs through the rice and check the seasoning. Serve immediately.

my way

food writer Tom Norrington-Davies

Hooray! Camp, as in an actual row of tents, is back! Everyone is buying tents, from lonely fell walkers to extended families. All of which leads me to this muddy booted collection of recipes. I'm preparing you for the revolution. Imagine the campsite going the way of that other re-invented institution; the pub.

At 'gastro campsites' potato granules and spam would be confiscated on arrival, and campsite shops bulldozed into foraging patches (wild sorrel is the new rocket). Actually, I've always loved camping but never understood that slightly masochistic tendency to live on miserable food when outward bound.

Cooking under canvas needs to be simple, but any traveller will tell you that some of the best food in the world is the moveable feast; from Indian railway journeys to Caribbean beach shacks. The recipes are a nod to that kind of cookery. My motto is this: one burner stove equals one-pot cooking. Moreover, it needs to be fairly brick. Mess tins are great but the camp stove's best friend is a wok.

Hot Chocolate

Ingredients
(Serves 1)
Two large squares of
organic chocolate
Two tbsp of cream
Mug of full-fat milk

Method
Allow the chocolate squares to
melt over a low heat. Mix in the
cream, beating quickly with a
spoon. Add the milk slowly, still
beating all the time. When the
hot chocolate is hot, but not
boiling, pour it back into the mug
and crumble a small piece of
chocolate into it.

Baked Banana

Method
Cut a banana through the skin and
flesh lengthways along the inside
curve of the banana. Gently stuff
the opening with chocolate and
marshmallows.

Wrap in foil and lay on hot coals for
five minutes. When you take it off,
you'll have a delicious pudding to
eat with a spoon.

Camp Treat

This utterly spoiling treat is from
Raffaella Barker and is ridiculously
simple, but gorgeous.

Put a tin of condensed milk in a pan
of boiling water. Allow it to boil for a
couple of hours. Open the tin and eat
the resulting toffee on sticks.

Smores

I'm English, so I feel wholly
unqualified to offer up an
American recipe, but here goes...

First, I'm reliably informed, you
need to find the perfect stick and
then whittle it until it has a sharp
point. Place your marshmallows on
the stick and roast them until they
are golden.

Then take a graham cracker
(digestive biscuit to the Brits)
and place squares of chocolate
(Hershey's, for authenticity)
on the cracker.

Put the toasted marshmallow
on top of the chocolate and add
another cracker, effectively making
a hot, gooey sandwich.

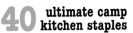

don't forget

40 **ultimate camp kitchen staples**

For the store cupboard hamper
Home-baked bread
Chocolate cake
Salt and pepper
Flour
Olive oil
Dried pasta
Selection of fresh herbs
Foil
Tinned tomatoes
Jar of clams
Good quality stock cubes
Rice
Ketchup
Peanut butter and Marmite
Jam and maple syrup
Tea, coffee and sugar

For the coolbox
Champagne
Quails' eggs
Scallops and cods' roe
Milk and cream
Butter and eggs
Sausages and bacon
Fish
Potatoes
Tomatoes
Onions
Cheese
Salad leaves
Rococo chocolates

74 fashion 80 beauty

style

However you're camping, it's possible to do it with real style. First you need to disregard any camping prejudices you may have. They have no place in your tent and should be left firmly at home. Once you begin to see camping as a blank canvas, you open up a world of magical possibilities. From the gorgeous yurts of Canvas Chic in France, to the space-age luxury of a Whitepod, with a vast array of options in between, camping has never been so good. The trick to making it work is to adapt entirely to life outdoors. It's possible to camp beautifully and stay warm without having to drop your standards. Follow a few simple rules and you'll have camping in style sewn up.

myway

Jodie Kidd on what she likes to take when she's camping

You can do the cool, grungy look. Getting dirty's OK – if you wear the right top and have clean hair then you can carry it off. It's important not to go too far with the grunge look. It shouldn't matter if you get a bit muddy – it'll just add to the look. Kate Moss does a good job of it – she looks amazing.

Trainers For when it's dry

Cool waterproofs Burberry does them and Stella McCartney's done some brilliant stuff for H&M

T-shirts Take a variety of them

Cashmere So insulating and keeps you warm

Cashmere socks Because they're warm and when walking they stop boots rubbing

Plus Brora jumpers, hats and gloves and silk underwear is a must

Luxury A Fired Earth rolltop bath!

Effortless Kate Moss shows how to do festival cool, here at Glastonbury

wearitout

Just because you're camping it doesn't mean you have to lose your sense of style. In fact, it's an excuse for a whole new look. It also gives you a reason to invest in lots of cashmere and utterly luxurious things that'll make you feel glamorous and cosseted at the same time.

Camping offers you the chance to let your fashion alter-ego out of the closet and have some serious fun with your wardrobe. Of course, you must keep warm and dry, but in perfect weather or when you're camping at a festival, you should let your imagination run riot.

Good looks for camping include 1950s sundresses, 1940s tea dresses, and Audrey Hepburn-style capri pants. If you have good legs that are tanned, then Wellington boots with a mini skirt or shorts can look fantastic.

One of the highlights of the fashion calendar is seeing what Kate Moss, Sienna Miller and the like will wear at Glastonbury. Each year Kate turns up looking utterly fantastic in some completely unexpected outfit. While designers may show their stuff on the catwalk, it's often on Glastonbury's muddy fields that fashion trends really begin.

Style is all about simplicity; wearing clothes appropriate to the occasion, not caring too much, and not slavishly following fashion. If you abide by these rules while in the field you'll look gorgeous and, importantly, feel comfortable. It's impossible to look stylish if you have a permanent grimace of discomfort on your face.

If you think about the most memorable festival outfits, they've actually been simple and practical. Sure, you need to have endless legs to be able to pull off a hotpants-and-boots combination, but whatever your shape by

style fashion

keeping it chic and simple and not looking as if you've tried too hard, you'll pull together a camping look that really works.

Accessories are really important. Often it's an amazing belt, pair of sunglasses or boots that make an outfit and, when at a festival or camping you can be truly frivolous. The sunglasses Sienna Miller wore at Glastonbury sparked a fashion frenzy as companies raced to copy them and get them on the shelves.

True style is effortless. The only time it's acceptable to look as if you've really tried is on your wedding day. For every other occasion in life paring down is always advisable. Self-consciousness is not an attractive look and, plastered on make-up in a tent can look a little silly.

If you're having a camping party, however, you should throw out the rulebook and be as glamorous as you like. Serious dressing-up is enormous fun wherever you are and there's something really intoxicating about wearing beautiful clothes in the great outdoors.

Camping allows you to have a lot of fun with your clothes and to wear things you might not normally at home. You do, though, need to be a bit practical and make sure that you stay warm.

A hat is vital when camping. I firmly believe that unless you play for the Mets or the Yankees you shouldn't wear a baseball cap. Try a stylish straw hat to keep the sun off your face. For the

boys, think Englishman abroad and for the girls a vintage straw hat with a beautiful fabric band always looks wonderful.

If you can't raid your granny's wardrobe then eBay or charity shops are a good place to look. In wet weather leather or waxed cotton cowboy hats are smart and it can get quite cold at night when camping so it makes a lot of sense to pack a cashmere or wool beanie.

Socks are an important piece of camping kit. Cashmere socks are luxurious and expensive, but a luxury worth investing in. They stop boots from rubbing but can be quite delicate. They are, however, perfect to wear in bed. It's a good idea to look for socks designed for the purpose, so if you're wearing wellies then buy some boot socks. If you plan to hike, buy some socks designed for heavy walking.

Jeans are great for light camping and festivals, but awful in the rain, as denim feels horrible next to the skin when wet. Camping jeans need to be soft and comfortable.

It's inexcusable to wear bad underwear. Admittedly when camping in bad weather, you may have to compromise on your outerwear, but underneath should be utterly perfect. If it's cold, then silk long johns will do the trick. If it's hot, be as girlie as you like. I think there's something rather charming about wearing gorgeous lace under less than glamorous outerwear.

Pyjamas are a must when camping. Apart

Shades of style
Sienna Miller at Glastonbury
in the sunglasses that
caused such a stir

my way

**Alice Temperley packs some
of her camping essentials**

On my bed Mattresses, huge feather
sleeping bags and/or duvets

In my bags Soft towels, a bucket to
wash my hair in, face spray, bottle
of water, a toothbrush and lots of
Van Morrison CDs

Luxury items Mine would be a
free-standing bath outside the tipi

On my feet Wellies

Plus "In a tent I think you should
take your normal sleeping stuff
rather than sleeping bags. It's
much more comfortable if you
pretend it's your own bed"

Best foot forward
You'll be warm, comfortable and seriously hip
if you choose boots that are sheepskin lined like
the ones here

from the fact that you'll be chilly without
them, you'll also be pleased you wore them if
something drives you suddenly from your tent
in the middle of the night.

T-shirts are really important when camping
as they're perfect to wear in sunny weather, good
to use as an under layer when you're huddled
up in warm sweaters and are lightweight so
pack up really small.

Footwear is another area you simply have to
get right. Wellies should feature highly on your
must-have list and it's rather comforting to know
that it's possible to look gorgeous in them. Jodie
Kidd and Alice Temperley agree they're essential
for camping in Britain. If you plan to walk,
you'll need hiking boots or a good pair of
trainers. If you're not planning to walk very
far and the weather's good, then flip-flops or
Birkenstocks are a good camping staple.

Sweaters, too, are essential. I've probably
talked far too much about the benefits of
cashmere, but as you can now buy it at at very
affordable prices, it is worth considering as a
camping staple. Lambswool sweaters are a
good idea as well as they're soft and warm.

When the weather's good you can be as
glamorous as you like while camping. You can
channel your inner 1950s goddess, wear caftans
like Kate Moss did at Glastonbury, or go for a
more fairytale approach as Alice Temperley does.
"The clothes should be magical and ethereal,
sort of Arabian Nights," she says.

Pared-down chic
In the right hat, jacket and trousers,
you'll feel warm and comfortable

comeclean

10 beauty essentials you shouldn't leave home without

A travel-size beauty kit I love the one from This Works

Vaseline It has so many uses – from skin first-aid to lip gloss

Cleansing wipes Incredibly useful, so take more than you think you'll need

Toothpaste & toothbrush With clean teeth you can face anything

Anti-bacterial handwash One that doesn't need water

Moisturiser Because the weather can play havoc with the skin

Sun block Even if it doesn't feel hot, the sun can still do damage

Bottle of your favourite scent Because it's one thing you should never go without

Soap You'll always find somewhere to wash, even if it's in a stream

Cleansers & toners Even in the wild it's surprisingly easy

lookgood feelgood

It's actually surprisingly easy to stay looking gorgeous outdoors. Just keep things simple.

Just because you're camping you shouldn't let your beauty routine go entirely to pot. I'm not for a moment saying that you should get up in the morning and plaster the make-up on, more that just because you're living outdoors you shouldn't stop caring entirely.

Your beauty routine will be easier to follow if you put in a little preparation before you go. Get all your waxing done a couple of days before your trip so your skin's not too sensitive.

You might as well get your eyebrows done, too, as groomed brows make you look much better even if you haven't slept for three days and are covered in mud.

"For camping, wipes are the best things ever invented," says Jodie Kidd. "They're so handy and you can get all sorts. Cleansing ones, baby wipes and antibacterial ones. You just

Snow patrol
It's easy to look stylish,
whatever the weather

**Cool-hunter Will Higham with
some grooming tips for men**

Hydration
cream
The weather
can be really
rough on skin

Something for
your hair
Gel, gum or
wax, you
choose

Lip balm
Kiss her and if it's strawberry
flavour will take her straight back
to the sixth-form school trip

Foot cream
If you're planning to do any hiking

Deodorant
A man-against-the-elements type,
pine-scented with outdoors notes

Razor
If you're going for the clean-cut
look, use a cut-throat razor and
water boiled over the camp fire

Dog
Borrow a large breed, such as a
Deerhound, Pointer or Lurcher. It'll
help you look seriously cool

shove them in your bag and off you go. I also like all the mini products you can get.

"When I go camping I become obsessed with Boots and the mini Take-Away stuff they sell. Charles Worthington products are great. It can be fun preparing for a camping trip now you can get all of these things in small sizes.

"You don't need to overpile the make-up. You just need to look fresh. Being outside gives you that perfect rosy look anyway, so all you need is a bit of lip gloss and mascara."

Your toothbrush and toothpaste are two things you really don't want to forget. You can get travel-sized ones if space in your bag is an issue.

Keeping hair clean and tidy can be a bit of a problem. If it's long you can always put it up and whatever its length you can pop it under a hat. Alice Temperley takes a bucket in which to wash hers and I have a friend who insists the best way to keep your hair fresh when you can't wash it is by rubbing baby powder into your scalp, leaving it for a few minutes and then vigorously brushing your hair.

spacesage

The romance of camping is something lost on many people. Buried, no doubt, under layers of nylon and fears of sleepless nights, spiders and endless days with nothing to look forward to but a tin of baked beans and an evening scraping dried mud from boots. Camping is an art and a science and accessorising your space is part of the joy.

Picnic hampers look lovely and are space-saving, because you can keep all your plates, glasses and cutlery in one place and the hamper itself can act as a table. Wicker hampers are lovely and you can either buy them empty or with all you need already chosen for you. Vintage hampers are readily available on eBay and sometimes at car boot sales.

I know it's complicated, but I like to use proper china and glass when camping and have collected vintage china and sturdy glass from antique shops, markets and car boot sales.

Cutlery-wise, Cath Kidston and Emma Bridgewater have cutlery perfect for camping.

Scarves and beads look fabulous draped around the liner-rope in a tipi and can add a sense of romance to yurts, tents or campers.

Camping among piles of cushions can be gorgeously indulgent and practical too. Cushions are insulating, comfortable and add a splash of colour. Rugs, too, are good for similar reasons.

When it comes to lighting it's nice, if possible, to try to ban anything fluorescent as it gives out a harsh light. Gas lamps or candle lanterns are romantic and give out a much more relaxing and flattering light. Candles are also soothing. Tea-lights on a metal tray look gorgeous, but keep them away from anything flammable.

Outside, allow your personality to be on show. Hang balloons or ribbons from your tent. Bunting's my favourite; there's something so joyful about those small fabric triangles blowing in the wind.

Finishing touches
The attention to detail is simply stunning within this fantastic Canvas Chic yurt in France

sleeptight

Some of us are put off the idea of camping because of worries about being warm and comfortable when the time comes to turn in. It is perfectly possible, though, to do it in such style you may just get the best night's sleep ever.

Spending the night under the stars can be so exciting that sleep can sometimes take a while to come. Use this time for yourself and enjoy it for what it is: the chance to experience real peace without the hum of traffic or light pollution.

Take a notebook so you can jot down any thoughts you want to hold on to. Or keep a camp diary. If you take a Polaroid camera and a glue stick you can illustrate it. Make sure you've got a nice pen and use your neatest writing and you'll have something gorgeous to show your grandchildren.

Take a cashmere throw or a snug wool blanket to put round your shoulders while you're sitting up in bed. Also, make sure you pack some lovely pyjamas. Just because you're in the wilderness it doesn't mean you want to let standards slip!

The books you choose for a camping trip are important too. *Swallows and Amazons*, by Arthur Ransome, is an obvious choice, but brilliant nevertheless. *Love in a Cold Climate*, or for that matter anything by Nancy Mitford, is good. *Charlotte Sometimes*, by Penelope Farmer, is perfect, as is anything that reminds you of childhood.

Make sure you go to bed with a cup of herbal tea or real hot chocolate. Also, pack a really good pillow, some cashmere socks and, if the weather's cold, a woolly hat, too, to wear while you're sleeping.

Your bedding is a matter of choice. Sleeping bags are fine, but try to choose a cotton-lined one unless you're camping somewhere really cold as it'll be much more comfortable. Silk sleeping bags are remarkably cheap and much nicer than the nylon variety. Many people use proper bed

readinglist

Cool under-canvas books

Famous Five Adventure Collection
Enid Blyton

Swallows and Amazons
Arthur Ransome

Love in a Cold Climate
Nancy Mitford

Charlotte Sometimes
Penelope Farmer

Come Back Lucy
Pamela Sykes

Marianne Dreams
Catherine Storr

A Handful of Time
Kit Pearson

Tom's Midnight Garden
Philippa Pearce

The Woman in Black
Susan Hill

How I Live Now
Meg Rosof

The Moth Diaries
Rachel Klein

Hideous Kinky
Esther Freud

Seven Pillars of Wisdom
T E Lawrence

linen when camping and swear by it. Double sleeping bags can result in a bit of a tug-of-war during the night, so a duvet might be a better option. I also always use a fur thrown between my mattress and sheet as it makes life warmer and more comfortable.

What you sleep on is a matter of choice, too. Options include a bedroll, inflatable mattress or camp bed, all of which are available from camping shops. You could go natural and sleep on the grass in a sleeping bag. It's great for spotting shooting stars, but be prepared to wake up covered in dew.

Personally I need something comfortable to sleep on otherwise I'm utterly miserable. A good choice is a cowboy bedroll, which is made from real canvas and can be bought online. They're really comfortable, protective and look very cool too.

An iPod can help you drift off into a world of your own with soothing music or an audio book. Badger Sleep Balm is a real treat; it smells delicious and a small dab on your temples not only ensures a really good night's sleep, but I swear it also makes you dream.

One of the greatest joys of camping is a midnight feast. Among my favourite things are home-baked cookies and a glass of milk, Green & Black's or Divine chocolate and Ritz crackers. If I'm staying in a tipi, or somewhere I can cook without having to brave the cold, I love mushrooms on toast late at night.

The period between climbing into your bed and drifting off to sleep is the most magical time. Make sure you really enjoy it by packing yourself some indulgences that'll ensure you can't wait for night to fall…

playlist

Play these on your iPod at bedtime to help you drift off to sleep

Rush of Blood to the Head Coldplay

La Femme D'Argent Air

Stella by Starlight
Stan Getz and
Chet Baker

If I Should Lose You
Hank Mobley

The Shining
Badly Drawn Boy

When
it's Sleepy
Time Down South
Louis Armstrong

Fugitive Motel Elbow

Sleep Alone Moby

Turn Your Lights Down Low Bob Marley

Lay Lady Lay Bob Dylan

I'll Close My Eyes Jimmy Smith

Willow Weep For Me Stanley Turentine

Loose Fit Happy Mondays

Waltz for Koop Koop

Georgia Ray Charles

While My Lady Sleeps Chet Baker

90 love 96 friends 100 festivals

great
escape

Once you make the decision to go on an outdoor adventure, you never look back. Sleeping out offers an unparalleled sense of freedom and a holiday that's so far removed from real life that you're bound to come back refreshed, recharged and somehow more grounded. Whether you're going with friends, someone you love, or with your children, camping opens up a world of possibilities and an experience you'll never forget.

106 kids   **112** garden camping

two'scompany...

You love each other madly and so what could be more exciting? The two of you cosseted under canvas listening to music and canoodling under the stars.

There are few things as romantic as spending the night under canvas with someone you love. The sense of togetherness that being in confined quarters brings is second to none. If you don't live together, then this is your chance to play house. You get to indulge in domesticity, but in a magical setting.

If you do live together, then you get time to simply be with each other away from the hum drum. Keeping romance alive when you share a gas bill can be much harder than it was when you only saw each other once a week.

Whatever your circumstances, camping as a couple is brilliant. It's intimate, romantic and whatever happens you can't fail to feel close. If things go wrong then there's a real sense that it's the two of you against the world and when things go right it's pure bliss.

To a certain degree the stage of your relationship will dictate the sort of place you want to stay. I do know one couple who ended up camping on their first date together. They're still going strong after five years, but personally I wouldn't recommend it.

If you're a very new couple then camping provides a real getting-to-know-you experience. It's a good idea to have a chat about a few things before you set off. If you're utterly phobic about spiders, then for goodness sake tell your partner otherwise you'll be screaming blue murder and pointing wildly, while he stares at you as if you've gone completely bonkers.

If you've been together for a while and are looking for something really romantic to do together, then Canvas Chic's site in the South of France is a brilliant place to go. They have beautifully built yurts, which are as luxurious as a five-star hotel room. Or, Vintage Vacations on the Isle of Wight who offer the unique experience

Winter wonderland
There are few places as glorious
to camp at as Whitepod, found at
an altitude of around 5,000ft in
the Swiss Alps

of camping in a vintage Airstream trailer. This kind of trip allows you to indulge any 1950s fantasies you may have and is enormous fun.

If you're looking for a really glamorous camping experience – perhaps for a honeymoon or anniversary– then Longitude 131° at Ulluru is amazing. It's so posh that it's a member of the Small Luxury Hotels of the World Group and the tents have to be seen to be believed.

Wherever you decide to camp and whether you're in the lap of luxury or halfway up a mountain in a two-man hike tent, the most important thing to remember is to indulge one another. After all, you've chosen to escape from the world together, so you might as well have a delicious time while you're away.

Make a pact that you'll keep technology out of your space. If you take a mobile phone, keep it strictly for emergencies. No sneaking off to pick up messages and allowing the real world to crash into your tranquillity.

Spend your time discovering or rediscovering each other. Some of the games listed in the campfire section are a great way of learning things about each other. And the simple act of getting back to nature and enjoying simple things together often acts as a catalyst for opening up and getting closer.

Treat your space as a boudoir. Ban nylon sleeping bags and fluorescent torchlight. Instead use a tea light lantern which gives out a softer altogether more romantic light. Whatever you do, don't sleep in that oversized, faded t-shirt that should have been thrown out years ago; crisp cotton pyjamas are more attractive. Camping in a tipi is seriously romantic as you can allow the fire to burn all

truelove

15 ways to find romance under the stars...

Don't camp on a first date

Watch the sunset together

Go camping on your honeymoon

Use fab bed linen, not sleeping bags

Share fondue in bed

Make your own road movie – hire a camper van and head off with no firm plans

Write wishes on pieces of paper and burn them on the campfire

Tell ghost stories to each other. Fear, apparently, is an aphrodisiac

Wash each other's hair in a bucket and dry off around the fire

For a special gift, buy her a tipi

Nurture each other. Cook lovely food and tuck each other up in bed

Be the one to get up to close the tipi smoke flaps when it rains

Propose under canvas

Dance in the rain together

Sleep in a beach hut and wake up to the sound of the waves rolling in

great escape love

night and, with the smoke flaps open, you have a gorgeous view of the stars. The expanse of white is very calming and it's lovely to be able to walk on grass while undercover.

Make sure you camp somewhere beautiful. When you've nothing to do all day but be together, it's infinitely nicer if the setting is gorgeous too. Go for long walks and find isolated places to stop for lunch. Cook lavish suppers in the evening and share fondue midnight feasts while looking for shooting stars.

Romantic camping shouldn't be confined to summer. Sleeping under the stars in winter can be gorgeous. If the weather's chilly, you'll want to spend a lot of time under cover, which means hours of snuggling up.

If you're confined to base by bad weather or gripped by that delicious feeling of just not wanting to move, then reading ghost stories aloud can be enormous fun, as can playing games.

If you're going to stay somewhere with a ready-pitched structure, and so don't have a huge amount to carry, it can be more of an adventure to go by train. It means that you can both relax and neither of you has to worry about map reading. If you're in a camper van or RV and are going to be travelling around, it can be fun to stick a pin in the map with your eyes closed and see where you end up.

Keep a scrapbook of your trip. If you end up together forever, then you'll have a truly special memento of your trip. If you break up, you'll have something to sob over or burn on your next campfire. Either way, it's worth recording it properly.

The most important thing to remember is to indulge one another. After all, you've chosen to escape from the world together, so have a delicious time while you're away.

Start of the adventure
Travelling provides an opportunity
to discover things about one another

lovesongs

15 **romantic tracks to
cuddle up to in your tent**

Blue Moon Billie Holiday

Summertime Herbie Hancock

Wild is the Wind Nina Simone

A Kiss to Build a Dream On
Louis Armstrong

Have You Met Miss Jones?
Frank Sinatra

Sweet Thing Van Morrison

We're All the Way Eric Clapton

Riverman Nick Drake

Slave to Love Bryan Ferry

Makin' Whoopee Louis Armstrong

Dead and Lovely Tom Waits

He'll Have to Go Bryan Ferry

Nothing Compares to You
Stereophonics

Do Nothing 'Til You Hear from Me
Mose Allison

Roadtrip Black Car

friendsforlife

Going on a camping trip with friends is a real bonding experience. By leaving the city behind and tackling the great outdoors together you're sure to have an adventure that'll put the Famous Five to shame.

This is cool camping proper. What could be better than a group of your closest friends in a field, with great music, delicious food and wine and a roaring campfire? In fact, if you're new to camping this is probably the best way to start. It doesn't matter if you forget something, as someone else will be able to lend you whatever it is you need.

Camping as a crowd is a bit like having a mini festival all of your own. If possible go somewhere you'll have all to yourselves. There are lots of places where you can rent a site exclusively. These range from simple fields with absolutely no frills, to super-luxury tipi villages with a whole host of modern conveniences.

Larger campsites will often allow you to rent an entire field within the site or at least a pretty contained space. I once camped in Oxfordshire and the most organised bunch of people I've ever come across pitched up in the next field. There were about 20 of them. Of course they had lots of tents and paraphernalia, but the most impressive thing was their camp kitchen. Under the sort of canopy more often found in suburban gardens, they had an incredibly professional set-up. Fold-up tables were unfolded and they had a food prep area, storage shelves, cool bags and equipment that would be impressive in any domestic kitchen.

It's important to get together before you go and discuss expectations. This doesn't have to be a heavy and boring session. It's best done over a bottle of wine and can save a lot of heartache later. If you're after a true back-to-nature experience where you escape civilisation for a week and live off the land and your friends

like*minded*

10 tips on staying friends in the great outdoors...

Only go with people you like – tents are no place for friends who drive you mad or make you feel inferior

Create a kitty for camp essentials

Don't take a new partner camping with friends if they've never met

Make sure one of your group can play the guitar or harmonica

Find a camping spot where your group can take over the entire space. Then you won't have to worry about noise levels

If camping in tents, completely erect one first, so if it rains you'll have somewhere to shelter

Get the campfire going early and let everyone cook their speciality

Write a rota for jobs

Be communal. This is not the time for labelling milk with your name

envisaged eating in five star restaurants and only returning to base to sleep, then you're heading for trouble. Talking about all aspects of the trip will ensure you have an enjoyable time.

I believe the fun of camping lies in not allowing the real world into your temporary oasis. Camping, for me at least, is about hearty breakfasts, long walks, afternoon naps and long, sociable campfire suppers with stories, singalongs and games. I think trips into the local town should be kept to a minimum and only for necessary provisions.

In a large group of people it's likely that everyone will have different skills and talents. Obviously it makes sense that if one of you is a brilliant cook and loves doing it then they should be in charge of food. Unfortunately, there are jobs that no one enjoys but that need to be done. For these it's only fair that you take turns, if you don't someone's going to end up grumpy and resentful.

Try to include in your group someone who's a brilliant guitar player. When you're cold and things are going wrong you'll need to sing to keep your spirits up. It's easier to sound tuneful if there's a guitar god strumming next to you.

When you're living communally, even if it's only for a few days, voting can be quite useful. As can drawing straws. It would, of course, become tedious if you applied these rules for everything. But for the big things it can be rather useful.

Allowing people privacy is important too. If there's a new couple with you they'd probably like to sneak off for some time alone. It's best to operate a knock before entering policy. If you're camping in separate tents you probably don't want to walk in and find your best friend's boyfriend changing. Or worse.

playlist

10 classic tracks to get the crowd going

Jammin' Bob Marley

Wake Up Boo The Boo Radleys

I'm Sticking with You Velvet Underground

Freebird Lynyrd Skynyrd

Sing Travis

Wild World Jimmy Cliff

Mr Blue Sky Electric Light Orchestra

You've Got a Friend Donny Hathaway

You're a Hurricane, I'm a Caravan World Party

Good Vibrations The Beach Boys

fieldsofdreams

With summer comes the excitement of festivals. The atmosphere is unique and listening to live music under the sun or stars is something everyone should experience at least once.

The Monterey International Pop Festival, held in the US over three days in June 1967, marked a turning point in music history. Two years later, the legendary Woodstock was staged and music fans the world over developed a taste for the great outdoors.

Jodie Kidd has camped at Glastonbury and loved the experience.

"It's a different kind of camping because you don't really sleep," she says. "There are too many other things to do. It's amazing just being there. You can spend days walking in the different fields and seeing all the acts.

"I love the meditation field and seeing the fortune tellers. There's such a great vibe that you have a wonderful time, whether it's rain, shine, snow, whatever." Alice Temperley, too, loves the festival vibe. "It probably helps that I have been camping at Glastonbury since I was three as my parents make cider and brandy and have a big compound there every year. It's a real family affair, complete with a double-decker bus."

Most festivals have a number of stages, marquees and fields where you can do everything from listen to your favourite band through to get a massage or watch a film.

Due to the array of activities on offer, it's best to check the programme on the festival's website before you go. You'll be crushed if you miss something you really wanted to see, so it really does pay to be prepared. If you're going in a group, it's much more sociable to face your tents inwards. That way you can chat while keeping warm and dry. On the subject of keeping dry, if

Glastonbury's Emily Eavis has advice on doing festivals well

Stay warm Many people who go to festivals turn up unprepared. It can get really cold at night

Be prepared You really have to prepare for all types of weather

Don't take too much cash If there's a cashpoint, you might as well use it

Remember where you left your tent It's a good idea to customise your area with bunting, flags, totem poles – anything that helps you recognise where you're camped

Listen up One of the most magical things about Glastonbury is the sounds at night. From drumming to the hum of things. It's an arresting feeling going to sleep with the festival in the background

Crowd control
Joss Stone passes a phalanx of fans en route
to the stage at the Glastonbury festival

you're camping at a festival in the UK, you need to be aware that it may rain and keeping dry and clean will become a bit of an obsession. Wellingtons or hiking boots are a must. Rainwear is a good idea, too, as is a decent stack of spare clothes. It's an attractive idea to travel light, but in practice it can be miserable if you have no clean, dry clothes.

Each festival has its own rules. Some allow fires and barbecues, others don't. You'll need to check websites for details before you go. There's a pretty universal no-glass rule, so any drinks you take need to be in cardboard cartons, cans or plastic bottles.

The most important thing to take to a festival is an open mind. Most have tents or areas with different types of music and entertainment. Sure, you should check out your favourite bands, but also try something new. Often the best bands you'll see are those you don't already know.

Also, you'll meet loads of new people. A tip for girls, though: a standard festival chat-up line is 'I'll pitch your tent for you if you'll let me sleep in it'. It goes without saying that it's not a good idea to share a confined space with a complete stranger, who is going to smell dreadful in a day or so.

Get to know your neighbours – they're the ones who'll watch out for your tent when you're not there, and who'll lend you precious camping commodities such as wet wipes, water and loo roll. On the subject of going to the loo at a festival, it's hideous and nothing can change that. Some festivals have better facilities than others, but it's never going to be great.

Mostly, the advice is to grin and bear it. But some festivals are close to a town with a supermarket or pub. If that's the case it might be worth a quick trip. The other benefit is, of course, that they'll have hot running water… sheer bliss.

Emily Eavis says her childhood memories of the festival blur, "but I remember there being lots of action at the same time of year every year.

"My earliest clear memory is of when I was about five, just seeing this onslaught of people arriving. Glastonbury has changed a lot over the last 10 years. It's become accepted as a part of British culture."

While Emily's too busy working at the festival to camp all the way through, she does recognise the importance of the festival camping experience. "I always camp on the last night and I never do the middle ground of sleeping in a caravan or trailer. You've got to do it properly in a tent.

"The years when I was between 15 and 19 were big camping years for me. I did Wednesday to Wednesday. I'm not a luxury kind of person really. What I think of as luxury is probably a necessity. Wipes are essential, but after three days in a tent they become a luxury. I also think it's nice to have a proper duvet in a tent."

"When I played festivals I was always on a tour bus and then whisked off to hotels," says

great escape festivals

don't forget

22 festival essentials you must pack in your bag

Festival ticket (in waterproof cover)

Baby wipes and loo roll

Ear plugs/ear defenders

Wellingtons or hiking boots

Bin bags (101 uses!)

Sunglasses

Cash (lots of it)

Mobile phone

Matches or lighter

Spare batteries

Condoms

One clean outfit per day

Something to sleep in

Gaffer tape (you'll need it)

Fold-up chairs

Bag on wheels (it can be a long walk from the car park)

Cooking equipment (if you're the Jamie Oliver type)

Towels (and keep them dry)

Disposable BBQ (if you're allowed)

Torch (make sure it's working)

Painkillers (for hangovers)

Toothpaste and dental floss

Alex James. "But I have camped at Glastonbury. I had one night in a tent, one in a camper and one at Babington. I think it's great to stay in a marvellous hotel at the end of a camping trip. The thing about luxury is that it's great to step in and out of it."

Eating at festivals can be a bit of minefield. Lulu, from Beau Nosh, the company best known for providing scrumptious backstage food for events such as Glastonbury and the Big Chill, says that if you're switched on you can eat really well.

"Don't eat anything after 2am because it would have been sitting around for ages," she says. "Clean your hands with wet wipes before and after eating and take lots of money because food can be really expensive."

Early birds fare well on the food front. "If you get up early, you'll get a really good fresh breakfast to set you up for the day. Also, food can vary in quality, so check the bins next to the vendor. If they're full of uneaten food, then it's best to find another outlet."

The great thing about festivals is that there are so many different kinds so you can chose one that suits you. You'll experience a huge amount, meet loads of people, hear some great music and see some unbelievable sights, so don't forget to pack a disposable camera.

Sound and vision
Camping at a festival is a treat
for all the senses – you're sure
to hear amazing sounds and see
things you can't quite believe

playlist *

15 **classic tracks with a festival feel...**

There's no homework to be done, no room to tidy or piano to practice...

arewethereyet?

Children see camping as fantastic fun, their active imaginations ignited by the idea of Swallows and Amazons-style adventures in the great outdoors.

Camping with children can be truly magical. They see the whole thing as a huge adventure and instantly get into the spirit of it. If you camp somewhere deserted, their imaginations are so good they believe they're the last people on earth. If you camp somewhere busier, they instantly make lots of friends and spend the entire trip together, only coming back to base when they want to be fed.

During a camping trip, everyday rules go out of the window. There's no homework to be done, no room to tidy or piano to practice. For a child, camping represents unparalleled freedom.

It's also an escape from the electrical fog that many children seem to spend their lives in. I believe hand-held electronic games should be banned from camping trips and good old-fashioned fun should be the order of the day.

There are many brilliant places to camp with children and it can be a tough choice. Obviously there are lots of sites that have things like swimming pools and holiday clubs. The price you pay for these, though, is that they tend to be very large and busy and often have static caravans as well as tents and motorhomes. I think it's much better to find a small campsite that doesn't stretch to such modern conveniences, or to go out of season. Some of the larger campsites do have quiet areas and fields set aside purely for tents.

Avoid at all cost campsites that have a disco or nightclub on site. The pounding of drum and

great escape kids

✱ playlist

10 classic tracks to feed the children...

Teach Your Children Well
Crosby, Stills & Nash

Hey Mr Tambourine Man
Bob Dylan

You Are My Sunshine
Bryan Ferry

Daydream Believer
Four Tops

Here Comes the Sun
The Beatles

Ain't Nobody Here But Us Chickens
Louis Jordan

What a Wonderful World
Louis Armstrong

Isn't She Lovely
Stevie Wonder

Livin' Thing
Beautiful South

Come on Eileen
Dexy's Midnight Runners

This is to certify that

....

has achieved first place

in the category of

bass at 2.30am is nothing short of torture when you have a child who's fractious from lack of sleep.

Small children can sometimes be a bit nervous about new experiences. Before you go on a camping trip it's a good idea to practice for a night in the garden. This allows them to experience it close to the safety of home. It also gives you a dry run when it comes to putting up a tent. Taking familiar things with you, such as favourite toys and their own pillows, can make them feel much more secure. Also, it's a good idea to show them pictures of where you'll be going. This'll help to build the sense of anticipation and excitement. Having said all of this, I've never met a child who doesn't take to camping almost instantly.

The most important thing with children is to make sure they're dry, warm and entertained. I actually think it's easier to keep them happy when camping than it is when you're at home, because you can give them your full attention. It's also really important to make sure it's as warm and comfortable as possible for them. Nothing spoils a camping trip more than whinging and nobody whinges more than an uncomfortable child. Filling the tent with cosy rugs and blankets makes bedtime a dream.

It's also a good idea to give children their own space. Even if you're camping in the smallest of tents, they can still have a bit to call their own. Here they can keep all their things and 'play house' in their own way.

Blissful places for children include tipi villages. They are extremely child-friendly and offer a world of make-believe for children of all ages. Campsites that are nothing more than a field are also good, because they are reassuring to parents as they make it easy to

Sign of the times
Children love camping and it's easy to get them involved with fun games, such as this competition for the best decorated tipi

keep an eye on the children. In fact, anywhere there is a small community, such as a site full of yurts or Airstreams, are good as kids enjoy meeting other people who are doing the same thing. My own boys once got rather competitive about who built the best campfire, us or the people in the tipi next door.

Being in a tent with children allows the family to become a democracy. Rafaella Barker, who often takes her three children camping, agrees:

"It's a communal thing," she says. "There's no leader, you're all just surviving. You find that everyone has a hidden skill. You discover primitive bits about yourself and you unearth things about your children. Whether it's their ability to identify different birdsong or point out a shooting star or finding they can cook really well, there's always something. Also there's something really special about seeing the dawn with your children. It recaptures the magical feeling of when they're new born and you're up at first light with them."

Outdoor life is incredibly exciting for children and it's enchanting to watch them engage with nature. From bug-hunting to naming stars or collecting fir cones for the fire to watching rabbits, there's always something to keep them amused. Lying in bed at night and asking them to identify the sounds of nature is both educational and amusing and, as long as you know your plants, allowing them to do a bit of foraging for the pot is bound to thrill them. It's amazing how children will try new foods if they've had a hand in gathering or preparing them.

Wherever and however you camp with children, you know that they'll remember it for life and it'll shape how they spend holidays with their own children.

don't forget

Leave these at home at your peril

Favourite bedtime toys

Things to divert them from tantrums

Baby wipes – things could get dirty

Books to read by torchlight

A tuck box each filled with their favourite foods

The pillow from home – good if they get nervous sleeping away

Badger Balm – to help them get off to sleep

Flashlight for security and fun

Plenty of clothes

Wellingtons – good for splashing in

Antiseptic, wipes and plasters

Board games and playing cards

Stories on iPod or tape

Drawing stuff – they can create their own masterpieces

Binoculars – for spotting wildlife and grown-ups

Fold-up telescope

First aid kit – you never know

Football – to tire them out

Softball and bats and cricket set

Disposable camera and notebook

10 tips to make garden camping seriously stylish

Only venture back to the house when strictly necessary

There is no such thing as too much bunting, so use it with abandon

Candles in coloured glass jars look gorgeous

Cook and eat all of your food outside

Make sure you turn the phones off so you can't hear them ringing from your hideaway

Take furnishings from the house to make yourselves as cosy and comfortable as possible

If possible, site your garden camp away from the house so you can pretend you're somewhere far away

Have a garden sleepover where everyone camps

Although you're probably only metres from your back door, pretend it's at least 50 miles away

Garden heaters allow you to stay out longer and are well worth the investment

closetohome

You don't have to travel miles to enjoy the thrill of camping in style or wait until you next have time to go away. In fact, why not camp in your garden straight away?

When life gets a bit stressful and you're feeling under siege from the phone and email it can be lovely to have a bolt-hole in the garden. Tipis and yurts are popular for garden camping as are shepherd's huts or even Airstream trailers. You can be really creative with garden camps. Friends of mine in Devon have created a natural tipi by erecting the poles and growing honeysuckle on camouflage netting.

One of the great things about creating a garden escape is that you don't have the worries associated with camping away from home. Weight isn't an issue as you won't have to carry anything too far, so you can indulge your fantasies all the way and even have a full-size bed in your outdoor haven.

Garden camps also make ideal dens for children, or can act as a spare room if your house is overflowing with guests.

If you fancy turning your garden or a nearby field into an under-canvas party venue, there are lots of companies who'll come and erect tipis, yurts or tents for your event and then come and take them all away again.

great escape garden camping

Emma Bridgewater loves camping in the garden. "We've even dragged a mattress onto the lawn because it was a beautiful night with amazing stars. With warm bedding, it's a great way to sleep out."

Children adore camping in the garden. It's a very safe adventure and is particularly reassuring for small children who may worry about going to the loo in the night or suddenly wanting something from their bedroom. It's also a great way of testing if you're the camping type. If you're unsure you could always borrow a tent from a friend, or be really adventurous and sleep out without anything between you and the stars. Waking up in the summer and instantly seeing the sky can be truly humbling.

myway

Kim Wilde on why garden camping is seriously chic

We've built a log cabin in the garden and planted trees around it, so we can pretend we're in the middle of nowhere

Even in your own garden you must have a campfire

Create a living willow den in the garden. It won't be waterproof, but will be great for camping in on summer nights

Plant a vegetable patch. Peas and raspberries are good

Grow herbs too. Grab a handful of rosemary and throw it on the fire

Keep warm and dry and enjoy really good food

A garden tree house is great to camp out in. We have one built into a willow tree and the branches are wrapped around it

Sing your own songs or listen to something laid back and ethereal, such as Travis, Blue Nile or Rufus Wainwright

116 style   118 destinations

listings

Want to buy a tipi, rent a yurt, find a festival, arrange a party under canvas, buy cool clothes for camping, go on a super-chic holiday or find out more about anything mentioned in this book? Here's the place to look.

fashion

7 for All Mankind
Great jeans that flatter and really last. Lots of styles, colours and sizes.
www.sevenforallmankind.com

Aigle
Totally sensible and perfectly funky coloured wellies that will help you stand out in the mud.
www.aigle.com

Akumuti
100% natural beauty products for the face and body.
www.akamuti.co.uk

Boden
Happy clothes for happy people. Good quality, functional and fashionable. Particularly good kids' wear.
www.boden.co.uk

Brora
Quality Scottish cashmere with a contemporary twist for men, women and children. Perfect for staying snug.
www.brora.co.uk

Converse
Will never go out of fashion. Each year they launch new colours and patterns, but you can't go wrong with navy blue or white.
www.converse.com

Driza-Bone
Great coats, hats and more for keeping dry in the great outdoors. **www.drizabone.com.au**

Edun
Gorgeous clothes with a conscience from Ali Hawson and Bono. **www.edun.ie**

Howies
Environment-conscious clothing that looks great too.
www.howies.co.uk

Hunter
Country classic wellingtons, as well as newer cooler colours.
www.wellie-boots.com

Hush
Gorgeous pyjamas, sweaters, sheepskin boots and more. Perfect for keeping warm and staying stylish.
www.hush-uk.com

Loomstate
100% organic cotton jeans which look fantastic and don't damage the environment.
www.loomstate.org

Old Town
Old Town makes the most glorious clothes. The company produces just 50 garments per week, everything made to order from English fabrics.
www.old-town.co.uk

Orla Kiely
Adorable boots, bags, clothes, umbrellas and lots more. All in the delicious Orla Kiely prints.
www.orlakiely.com

Pachacuti
Fair-trade hat specialist selling loads of classic and funkier versions, as well as all sorts of other hats.
www.panamas.co.uk

Portobello Road Market
One of the most famous markets in the world and full of brilliant things.
www.rbkc.gov.uk

Temperley London
Utterly amazing clothes, perfect for glamorous under-canvas parties.
www.temperleylondon.com

Toast by Post
My favourite online shop. Packed full of amazing clothes, footwear and other adorable items.
www.toastbypost.co.uk

Wellie Art
Stylish wellingtons and brilliant umbrellas to ensure you stay dry in the field.
www.wellieart.co.uk

style

Aga Cook Shop
Brilliant for cast-iron pans, kettles, grill pans and general cookware. Well-made, durable products that should last a lifetime. www.agacookshop.co.uk

Amaroni Homeware
Quirky and useful kitchen and household equipment. www.amaroni.com

Apple
For the best laptops (great to watch DVDs under canvas on) iPods and much more. www.apple.com

Cath Kidston
Good one-stop shop if you're new to chic camping. Gorgeous clothes, picnic stuff, camping equipment and more. www.cathkidston.co.uk

Diptyque
Brilliant scented candles and, if you're looking for a scent that's perfect for the great outdoors, then Philosykos is gorgeous. www.diptyque.tm.fr

Divertimenti
Hundreds of must-have products. Perfect place to equip your camp kitchen. www.divertimenti.co.uk

Emma Bridgewater
Beautiful ceramics and textiles which instantly cheer. The large mugs are perfect for hot chocolate round the fire. www.emmabridgewater.co.uk

Fired Earth
Gorgeous paints to help brighten up outdoor space and fab flooring perfect for yurts & tipis. www.firedearth.com

Garden Trading
Gorgeous kitchen and gardenware, innovative lighting solutions, traditional barbecues and much more. www.gardentrading.co.uk

Gibson guitars
Arguably the coolest guitars, with the range including wonderful acoustics ideal for campfire nights. www.gibson.com

House & Garden
Great range of products that are both stylish and practical, particularly useful outdoor and kitchen items. www.house-and-garden.co.uk

Labour & Wait
Timeless, functional products which look fantastic. The enamelware is beautiful and available in pretty pastel shades. www.labourandwait.co.uk

Latin Percussion
Great source for percussion needs. Colourful bongos and congas. Perfect for round the campfire. www.lpmusic.com

Odd Limited
Quirky and adorable, with an amazing range of garden furniture, camp beds, clothes, fabrics and much more. The website is a real Aladdin's cave. www.oddlimited.com

The Old Apothecary
Online shop selling traditional sweets, toiletries, remedies and housewares. www.oldapothecary.co.uk

Roberts radios
Portable, worldband, clock radios, digital and more. Simply the most stylish around. www.robertsradio.co.uk

Rosanna Inc
Gorgeous, girlie tablewear. Perfect to use while playing house in the great outdoors. www.rosannainc.com

Vestax
Ingenious portable record players so you don't have to leave your vinyl at home. www.vestax.com

The White Company
Gorgeous things that will make any camping trip truly stylish. www.thewhitecompany.com

where to stay

Belle Tents

Camp at Owl Gate, two and a half acres of gardens on the edge of Bodmin Moor. Gorgeous medieval-style tents, each camp equipped with its own kitchen. There's also a bar tent and a campfire area.
www.belletentscamping.com

Bucks on the Brazos

Based in Texas, this campsite offers different packages so you can choose how luxurious your stay is. Camp in your own tent or RV or in their luxury two-room tent cabins.
www.buckbrazos.com

Canvas Chic

A dozen amazing yurts in French paradise. Chic bathrooms, with shared kitchen tent. This is camping in serious comfort.
www.canvaschic.com

Chattooga River Resort

Near Clayton, Georgia, here you can camp in your own tent, but enjoy room service. Described as decadence in the wilderness and bordered by more than 88,000 acres of National Forest, this really is the great outdoors.
www.sockemdog.com

Cornish Tipi Holidays

40 tipis on a delightful site with a lake stocked with rainbow trout. Stay in the tipi village or separate spacious clearings. Couples and families only.
www.cornish-tipi-holidays.co.uk

Costanoa

In Southern California you can camp in your own tent or RV, or camp in one of their canvas cabins. Massages, delicious gourmet deli and relaxing spa on site.
www.costanoa.com

Deepdale Farm

Two gorgeous tipis on a quiet, family-friendly site in North Norfolk. Or hire an entire field, complete with barn where you can hire tipis or bring your own tent.
www.deepdalefarm.co.uk

Devon Yurt Holidays

Gorgeous yurts on a Devon smallholding. Organic food, amazing countryside and farm shop.
www.devonyurtholidays.co.uk

Hoopoe Safaris

Gorgeous tents with en-suite shower rooms and solar power. As well as the main camps there are smaller wilderness concessions. Seasonal and smart ecotourism award-winner.
www.hoopoe.com

Idaho Parks

Yurts and cabins in a beautiful park setting.
www.idahoparks.org

Indian Himalayas

Camp in the Himalayas in tents that give a new meaning to luxury. Spectacular and luxurious, but also offering a low-impact, sustainable tourism experience.
www.colours-of-india.com

Kooljaman

Award-winning Aboriginal-owned wilderness camp. Stay in safari tents, dome tents, beach shelters or cabins. Or take your own shelter and set up camp in one of the powered or unpowered pitches.
www.kooljaman.com.au

Koyote Ranch

A resort in the beautiful Texas Hill Country, where you can camp in tents, lodges or RVs. Great food and gorgeous scenery.
www.koyoteranch.com

Longitude 131°

5-star luxury in Kata Tjuta National Park. Gorgeous tents with private bathrooms and all the

extras you'd expect at a seriously chic hotel. Children over 15 welcome.
www.longitude131.com.au

Mashatu

Amazing camping in Botswana with some of the most exciting game viewing in Africa. Blissful tents and facilities and by camping here you're helping the game reserve with much-needed funds.
www.mashatu.com

Okavango Tours & Safaris

To travel through Kenya with your own safari guides and to stay in your own private camp is unsurpassed. Comfort, safety and exclusivity are the key ingredients for this type of safari and it is an unforgettable experience.
www.okavango.com

Paws Up

Camp in glorious style in Tent City. Feather beds, in-tent spa treatments and hot running water in delightful bathrooms. Fabulous food and great activities.
www.pawsup.com

Pot-a-Doodle Do Wigwam Village

Sleep in a wooden wigwam in rural Northumberland. On-site facilities include a shop, restaurant, showers, campfires and an interactive art centre.
www.northumbrianwigwams.com

Ride Worldwide

Brilliant riding holidays across the world where you can explore remote wilderness and sleep under canvas.
www.rideworldwide.co.uk

Snowed Inn

Environmentally sustainable luxury yurt space in 11 private acres on an Idaho mountain.
www.snowedinnmccall.com

Tipi West

Camp in tipis by the coast in Wales. A fantastic festival vibe, with plenty of acoustic instruments and real

campfires. This is a chilled-out place to camp.
www.tipiwest.co.uk

Vintage Vacations

Three refurbished Airstream trailers on a farm on the Isle of Wight. Cool, quirky and utterly chic with a distinctly vintage accent.
www.vintagevacations.co.uk

Whitepod

High-tech eco camp for just 10 guest, around 5,000ft up in the Swiss Alps. Unique place to camp with delicious food and indulgent massages.
ww.whitepod.co.uk

Wild Adventures in Scotland

Camp in the remotest parts of Scotland's Highlands and Islands with Wild Adventures. You won't be pampered,

but you'll see some of the most beautiful scenery.
www.wild-adventures.co.uk

Wilderness Safaris

Life-changing trips in amazing locations and at simply gorgeous camps.
www.wilderness-safaris.com

Wilson Island

On the Great Barrier Reef, Wilson Island is like paradise and with fantastic tents and brilliant food this is true camping luxury.
www.wilsonisland.com

Yurt Ski

Camp in a fabulous yurt and ski in the Southern Swan Mountain Range of Western Montana.
www.yurtski.com

Yurt Workshop

Relaxing yurt holidays in Andalucia. Beautiful yurts, comfortable beds and cooking facilities.
www.yurtworkshop.com

festivals uk

All Tomorrow's Parties
Camber Sands, Sussex. Arty, out-there festival based in a holiday camp so you sleep in chalets. **www.atpfestival.com**

Bestival
Award-winning, super cool festival on the Isle of Wight. One of the places to be seen. **www.bestival.net**

Big Chill
Eastnor Castle, Herefordshire. Garden party feel, hot showers and cocktail bars, great music, art trail. **www.bigchill.net**

Big Green Gathering
Cheddar, Somerset.
Biggest event for those who care about environmental issues. Five days of music, entertainment and workshops. **www.big-green-gathering.com**

Carling Weekend Reading Festival
Reading, Berkshire. Young, rock 'n' roll, with great bands. **www.meanfiddler.com**

The Carling Weekend Leeds festival
Leeds, West Yorkshire. Mirror festival of Reading. Same weekend, same bands, different running order. **www.meanfiddler.com**

Download
Donington Park. Young crowd, loud music and fun. Festivals Ozzy Osbourne-style. **www.downloadfestival.co.uk**

Endorse-it-in-Dorset
Dorset. Cool music, kids field, workshops and a diverse range of acts on all stages. **www.lgofestivals.com**

Glastonbury
Pilton, Somerset. Probably the most famous festival. Certainly the coolest. **www.glastonburyfestivals.co.uk**

Global Gathering
Long Marston, near Stratford on Avon, Warwickshire. Dance festival with cutting-edge production values and a carnival atmosphere. **www.globalgathering.co.uk**

Green Man Festival
Hay-on-Wye, Wales. Small but perfectly formed festival on the Welsh Borders. **www.thegreenmanfestival.co.uk**

Isle of Wight Festival
The most famous British festival of the 60s was banned by parliament until 2002 and is now back with the coolest line-up of bands. **www.isleofwightfestival.org**

Lost Vagueness
Various locations. First seen at Glastonbury, Lost Vagueness must be seen to be believed. Now at many festivals including their own. **www.lostvagueness.com**

T in the Park
Perth, Kinross. Scotland's biggest music festival. Big name bands and a great party atmosphere. **www.tinthepark.com**

Truck Festival
Abingdon, Oxfordshire. Micro-Glastonbury which started in 1998. Cool, kitsch vibe with great music and entertainment. **www.truckfestival.org**

Wickerman Festival
East Kirkcarswell, South-west Scotland. Scotland's alternative festival born out of the desire to create the lost counter-culture vibe. **www.thewickermanfestival.co.uk**

Womad
Various locations round the world. World music, dance and arts. Family orientated, with multiple stages and hands-on workshops. **www.womad.org**

festivals usa

Austin City Limits
Austin, Texas. Good mix of big name, cool and new bands. No camping onsite, but lots of good places to pitch nearby. www.aclfestival.com

Bumbershoot
Seattle. Music, film, comedy, dance and theatre over four days. Great bands. No camping on site, but there are local sites. www.bumbershoot.org

Burning Man Project
Black Rock Desert , Nevada. Annual arts festival and temporary community based on radical self-expression and self-reliance. Totally out there and unlike anything else. www.burningman.com

Coachella
Indio, California. America's Glastonbury. Big-name bands, cool camping and great festival vibe. www.coachella.com

Download USA
America's version of the UK festival. Loud and lots of fun. www.downloadfestival.co.uk

High Sierra Music Festival
Intimate festival nestled in Northern California's majestic mountain range. A unique four-day event featuring an eclectic and boldly creative span of music from bluegrass to funk. www.highsierramusic.com

Lollapalooza
Grant Park, Chicago, Illinois. Two-day festival with no onsite camping. Great music though and a party atmosphere. www.lollapalooza.com

cool extras

Camp Kerala
Luxury tented village available at some festivals. www.campkerala.com

eFestivals
Truly brilliant website with everything you need to know about festivals in the UK. Tickets, chatroom, up-to-the-minute news section, it's all there. www.efestivals.co.uk

Electric Picnic
Stradbally Hall, County Laois, Eire. Ireland's hippest gathering is worth a listing. Seriously cool boutique festival, great music, food and atmosphere. www.electricpicnic.ie

Festival Finder
This site lists an amazing 2,500 festivals in North America. Search by genre, bands, dates or location. www.festivalfinder.com

Fly Glastonbury
Love the idea of Glastonbury, but can't face compromising on comfort? This is for you. The best of the festival in serious luxury. www.flyglastonbury.com

PodPads
The new festival craze. You can rent one backstage or opt to buy your own. Stylish and functional, they really are a home from home. www.podpads.com

Yourope
The European Festival Association represents 35 festivals across Europe. You'll find lots of information on the site. www.yourope.org

kit guide

Aga Stoves
Wood-burning stoves, perfect for shepherd's huts, yurts and tipis. Great if you're setting up a garden camp.
www.aga-web.co.uk

American Caravans by Sarah Jane & Guy
The most fabulous American trailers and motorhomes. Including, of course, many Airstreams.
www.american-caravans.co.uk

Belle Tents
Beautiful tents to hire or buy. Stunning to look at and utterly gorgeous to sleep in.
www.belletents.com

Blacks
Outdoor experts, selling everything from tents to boots. Also offer activity days.
www.blacks.co.uk

Bruton Yurts
This company makes and sells a range of fantastically stylish yurts.
www.brutonyurts.com

Camping and Caravanning Club
Great site offering all sorts of technical advice on equipment. You can also become a member and book holidays through the club.
www.campingandcaravanningclub.co.uk

Cast-Iron Chimineas
Huge range of great looking, good-quality cast-iron chimineas.
www.castironchimineas.co.uk

Cath Kidston
Tents, sleeping bags, cool bags, picnic chairs and much more in gorgeous prints and fabrics.
www.cathkidston.co.uk

Cave & Crag
Specialists in climbing, camping and walking equipment, in fact, everything you need for an adventurous camping trip.
www.cave-crag.co.uk

Colorado Yurt Company
Amazing yurts and tipis for sale in America. True luxury and very beautiful.
www.coloradoyurt.com

Cotswold Outdoor
Tents, footwear, outerwear, camping stoves, gadgets and much more.
www.cotswoldoutdoor.com

eBay
Brilliant for picking up all sorts of camping bargains.
www.ebay.com

Field & Trek
Everything you need to camp in and with. A great range of climbing equipment.
www.fieldandtrek.com

Handmade Hammocks
Fair trade hammocks in all shapes and sizes. Lovely to look at and relaxing to hang about in.
www.handmadehammocks.co.uk

Hearthworks
Brilliant tipis and yurts to buy or hire. Also have tipis to hire at some of the festivals and some campsites.
www.hearthworks.co.uk

Hugh Lewis
All kinds of camping equipment for all kinds of trips, including tents, sleeping bags, mats and accessories.
www.camping-supplies-uk.com

Leatherman
An invaluable multitool. Part of the camping kit and colourful too. Don't leave home without one.
www.leatherman.co.uk

LPM Bohemia
Beautiful tents, marquees and crafted structures for hire. Indian and exotic, traditional and vintage tents, plus marquees and yurts.
www.lpmbohemia.com

Maglite
Robust, durable and reliable torches in lots of cool colours. One of camping's true essentials.
www.maglite.com

Millets
Equipment, clothing, tents (including items from the Cath Kidston range). Everything you need to camp.
www.millets.co.uk

Nokia
Classic, stylish phones.
www.nokia.com

The North Face
For all your outdoor needs, from tents to rucksacks. Stylish and functional products for camping anywhere.
www.thenorthface.com

Outdoor Gear
All camping equipment including mats, adventure packs, rucksacks, clothing and footwear.
www.outdoorgear.co.uk

Outdoor World
Great site with all the camping essentials and lots of search options. Choose tents by brand, berth or type.
www.outdoorworld.org.uk

Petzl
Keep your hands free with these brilliant head torches. Perfect for reading in the tent or finding your way to the loo at night.
www.petzl.com

Pod Caravans
Adorable, retro caravans in pastel colours with funky interiors to rent or buy.
www.podcaravans.com

Shelters Unlimited
Suppliers of authentic tipis, Bedouin and Berber tents and their furnishings.
www.tipis.co.uk

The Shepherd's Hut Company
Beautiful shepherd's huts, including the one pictured on page 27, with all the optional extras you can imagine.
www.shepherd-hut.co.uk

The Stunning Tents Company
As the name suggests, truly stunning tents to hire for parties, balls and events.
www.stunningtents.co.uk

Surplus & Outdoors
Online supplier of Army Surplus, camping equipment and outdoor supplies.
www.surplusandoutdoors.com

Swiftsilver
Direct supplier of T@B in the UK. Passionate and knowledgeable on all

things T@B.
www.swiftsilver.com

Tents Direct
Wide variety of tents including canvas and group types.
www.tents-direct.co.uk

The Tipi Company
Makes, hires out and sells stunning tipis in the UK. Also offers a tipi party service where they'll set up a tipi field for you.
www.thetipico.com

Tipi.co.uk
Makers of wonderful tipis, including my own. Many sizes and colours available. Delivery and erection included in prices.
www.tipi.co.uk

Victorinox
Makers of the classic Swiss Army knife. Available in loads of colours, including cute pink and the classic red.
www.victorinox.com

Weber
Barbecues in all shapes and sizes. The portable grills are great for camping.
www.weber.com

Win Green
Adorable children's play tents, sleeping bags, floor quilts and much more. Makes you wish you were six years old again.
www.wingreen.co.uk

Wolf Glen Tipis
Tipis to hire and buy. Also arrange workshops, from music sessions to communal art, based in tipis.
www.wolfglentipis.co.uk

Woodland Yurts
Gorgeous yurts and the company's owner is an authority, having written a book on the subject.
www.woodlandyurts.co.uk

World Tents
Makes and sells historical tents, tipis, yurts, geo domes and scout tents. All materials used are natural or recyclable.
www.worldtents.co.uk

credits & permissions

photography

My thanks to the following for contributing such inspiring images

Front cover
    Pia Tryde with kind permission of
    Cath Kidston and Millets
2 American Caravans Ltd
5 Tipi.co.uk
6 Emma Bridgewater
7 Garden Trading
8 Bruton Yurts
10 Fired Earth
11 Swiftsilver Caravans
12 Leatherman
14 Pia Tryde with kind permission of
    Cath Kidston and Millets
16 The North Face
17 The North Face
19 The Tipi Company
20 Tipi.co.uk; The Tipi Company
21 Tipi.co.uk; The Tipi Company
22 Canvas Chic
25 Canvas Chic
27 Vanessa Buchan; Odd Limited;
    Swiftsilver Caravans; Vintage Vacations;
    Garden Trading; Fired Earth; PodPad;
    Punchstock
29 The North Face; Millets
    Maglite; Boysstuff.co.uk
30 Petzl; Cath Kidston; Nokia; Zippo
    Toast by Post
31 Tyson Sadlo; The White Company
32 Garden Trading; Aga Cook Shop;
    Divertimenti; Aga Cook Shop
33 Divertimenti; Labour & Wait
34 Garden Trading
35 Cath Kidston; Divertimenti

36 Brora; Drizabone; Brora; Toast by Post
37 Boden; Roberts Radio; Gibson; Vestax
38 WellyArt
40 The Tipi Company
43 Fired Earth
45 Britain on View
46 Eastern Daily Press/Colin Finch
48 Britain on View
51 Britain on View
52 Corbis
54 Spiros Politis; Latin Percussion
55 Odd Limited
56 Punchstock
57 Emma Bridgewater
58 Garden Trading
60 Britain on View
63 ThinkVegetables.com
64 ThinkVegetables.com
65 Canvas Chic
66 ThinkVegetables.com
67 Divertimenti
68 ThinkVegetables.com
70 Odd Limited
72 Roberts Radio
74 Empics
77 Empics; Venetia Dearden
78 Toast by Post
79 Toast by Post
80 ThisWorks
81 Boden; William Higham
83 Canvas Chic
85 Toast by Post
86 Venetia Dearden
87 Apple

88 The North Face
91 Punchstock
92 Whitepod
95 Punchstock
96 Punchstock
98 Hohner
99 Punchstock; Apple
101 Emily Eavis; The Tipi Company
102 Britain on View
104 Zippo
105 Bestival; PodPads; Gibson
107 Boden
108 The Tipi Company
109 Boden
110 Cath Kidston
112 Weber
113 Odd Limited
114 The North Face
116 Aigle; Brora
117 Labour & Wait; Pachacuti
118 Belle Tents; Caravan Club
    of Great Britain
119 Wilderness Safaris; Whitepod
120 Venetia Dearden; The Big Chill
121 The Big Chill; WaterAid
122 Handmade Hammocks; The Big Chill
123 Victorinox; Win Green
124 Paws Up
126 Vintage Vacations
Back cover
    The Tipi Company;
    Toast by Post;
    Vintage Vacations;
    Gibson

acknowledgements

thank you

Here's where I get to gush on behalf of all those who helped in so many ways to make this book happen

There are always quite a few people involved in making a book happen, but this one has upped the ante and there's been a whole crowd. So, I'd like to say a huge thank you to the following…

My brilliant agent, Antony Topping; every author should have an agent as wise. Jenny Heller, who commissioned this book and has been hugely fun and inspirational to work with (even at 6am on a Sunday morning). Lisa John, my editor, who was soothing throughout, particularly when the deadline loomed large and I was panicking.

Everyone who contributed their thoughts, ideas, recipes, anecdotes and tales. They include (oh god, I hope I don't forget anyone) Raffaella Barker, Jodie Kidd, Tom Norrington-Davies, Hugh Fearnley-Whittingstall, Alice Temperley, Emily Eavis, Kevin McCloud, Will Higham, Cameron McNeish, Martin Miller, Wilfred Emanuel-Jones, Lucy Young, Mitchell Tonks, Emma Bridgewater, Kim Wilde and Alex James. I can't think of a more gorgeous or talented group of people.

The people who were there every step of the way. Tim, who worked incredibly hard to make the book look so gorgeous, and only shouted at me twice. Zofia, who is like a ray of sunshine in the office and had me in stitches every day.

Everyone who helped with this project by contributing gorgeous pictures. Pia Tryde, for allowing me to use her gorgeous picture on the cover. Venetia Dearden, who is as kind as she is talented. Cath Kidston, Emma Bridgewater, Toast, American Caravans, The North Face, Canvas Chic, Win Green, Garden Trading, Odd Limited, Boden, The White Company, Aga, Divertimenti, Fired Earth, The Tipi Company, Tipi.co.uk, Bruton Yurts, Swiftsilver, PodPads, Vintage Vacations, Maglite, Nokia, Zippo, Petzl, Labour & Wait, Brora, Hunter, Roberts Radio, Vestax, Gibson, Wellie Art, Latin Percussion, Think Vegetables, Whitepod, Britain on View, Bestival, Glastonbury Festival and Weber.

There are so many beautiful and useful things featured and if you want to find out where they're from, they are listed on the

acknowledgements

previous page. Company contact details are in the listings section starting on page 116.

I'm grateful to all those who worked so hard to get many of these images to me. Particularly brilliant were Ching Yick, from Flax PR, who surely must have thought I was stalking her, Ruth Bonser at Cath Kidston, who was an enormous help, and Ros at Creative Talent, who was great too.

Thank you to Phil Royle at Tipi.co.uk, who made my tipi and got me hooked on the whole camping thing in the first place. Greg Bramford, from The Tipi Company, has also been brilliantly helpful, knowledgeable and fun throughout. Ruth Lawson, from Canvas Chic, has been great fun to chat to.

A huge thank you to Tristan, who has been characteristically generous with ideas, contacts and morale-boosting efforts.

And finally to my adorable children, Lucie, Tatti, Jack and Toby, for being the best people in the world to camp with.

WaterAid

Worldwide, a child dies every 15 seconds from water-related diseases, a figure equivalent to 20 jumbo jets crashing each day.

This is why a percentage of the royalties from this book will go to WaterAid. The charity works to help some of the poorest communities in Africa and Asia provide themselves with a better quality of life through water, sanitation and hygiene education projects.

The charity, established in 1981, now helps more than 500,000 people every year and also seeks to influence water and sanitation policies on a global scale.

If you'd like more information on WaterAid, or would like to make a donation, you'll find them at:

WaterAid,
47-49 Durham Street,
London, SE11 5JD
Telephone 020 7793 4500
www.wateraid.org

About the author

Laura James is an author, journalist, food writer and magazine editor. She writes celebrity interviews and articles on fashion, food, trends, relationships, interiors and style.

Her writing has appeared in national newspapers and magazines. She is also a consultant to cool hunters The Next Big Thing, reporting on food, home and style trends. This is her fifth book.

When not frantically bashing out copy, Laura can be found in her North Norfolk garden, inside a glorious tipi surrounded by her gorgeous children, whipping up delicious food on a roaring campfire.